Greg Byrd, Lynn Byrd and Chris Pearce

Cambridge Checkpoint

Mathematics

Challenge Workbook

7

T0306653

CAMBRIDGE
UNIVERSITY PRESS

CAMBRIDGE
UNIVERSITY PRESS

University Printing House, Cambridge CB2 8BS, United Kingdom

One Liberty Plaza, 20th Floor, New York, NY 10006, USA

477 Williamstown Road, Port Melbourne, VIC 3207, Australia

314–321, 3rd Floor, Plot 3, Splendor Forum, Jasola District Centre,
New Delhi – 110025, India

103 Penang Road, #05-06/07, Visioncrest Commercial, Singapore 238467

Cambridge University Press is part of the University of Cambridge.

It furthers the University's mission by disseminating knowledge in the pursuit of education, learning and research at the highest international levels of excellence.

www.cambridge.org
Information on this title: www.cambridge.org/9781316637418 (Paperback)

First published 2017

20 19 18 17 16 15 14 13 12 11 10 9 8 7

Printed in Malaysia by Vivar Printing

A catalogue record for this publication is available from the British Library

ISBN 978-1-316-63741-8 Paperback

All Checkpoint-style questions and sample answers within this workbook are written by the authors.

Contents

Introduction

Welcome to Cambridge Checkpoint Mathematics Challenge Workbook 7

The *Cambridge Checkpoint Mathematics* course covers the Cambridge Secondary 1 Mathematics curriculum framework. The course is divided into three stages: 7, 8 and 9.

You can use this Challenge Workbook with Coursebook 7 and Practice Book 7. It gives you increasingly difficult tasks or presents you with alternative approaches or methods in order to build on your existing skills.

Like the Coursebook and the Practice Book, this Workbook is divided into 19 units. In each unit there are exercises on each topic that will develop and extend your skills and understanding in mathematics. This will improve and deepen your understanding of the units. At the end of each unit is a set of 'mixed questions' to help you check your knowledge and understanding.

If you get stuck with a task:

- Read the question again.
- Think carefully about what you already know **and** how you can use it in the answer.
- Read through the matching section in the Coursebook.

1 Integers

1.1 Negative numbers

1 Fill in the missing numbers.

a 9 + ... = 3 **b** –6 + ... = –10 **c** ...... + 5 = –5 **d** ...... + –5 = 7

2 Fill in the missing numbers.

a ...... – 5 = 9 **b** ...... – –5 = 9 **c** ...... – –8 = –6 **d** ...... –7 = –17

3 Fill in the missing numbers.

a 7 – ...... = 9 **b** 10 – ...... = 15 **c** 7 – ...... = –9 **d** –10 – ...... = 15

4 The sum of two numbers is 1.

The difference between the two numbers is 37.

Find the numbers. ...... and ......

5 –7, 3 and n are three numbers on a number line.

The three numbers are equally spaced on the line.

Find all the possible values of n. ....

6 Here is a new way to write the time:

Midday is 00*00.
Two hours AFTER midday is 02*00.
Three hours BEFORE midday is –03*00.

a Write these 24-hour clock times in the new way.

i 15:00 .... **ii** 08:00 .... **iii** 09:30 ....

b Write these times in the usual 24-hour clock.

i 05*45 .... **ii** −05*45 .... **iii** −10*15 ....

c The time now is −07*35. Write the time 12 hours later in the usual 24-hour clock.

....

1.2 Tests for divisibility

1 Here is a five-digit number with a missing digit: 35**?**84

The number is divisible by 3 but not by 9.

Find the possible values of the missing digit. ....

2 Find a test for divisibility by 15.

Hint: 15 = 3 × 5

Give some examples to show that your test works.

....

....

....

....

3 Find a test for divisibility by 18.

Give some examples to show that your test works.

....

....

....

....

4 **a** Find the smallest number that is divisible by 2, 3, 4, 5 and 6 ....

b What can you say about ANY number that is divisible by 2, 3, 4, 5 and 6?

....

1.3 Prime numbers

1 How many prime numbers are less than 100?

Circle the correct answer.

23 24 25 26 27

2 $35 = 5 \times 7$

35 is the product of TWO different prime numbers.

How many numbers less than 40 are the product of two different prime numbers?

....

Explain how you found your answer.

....

....

3 How many numbers less than 100 are the product of THREE different prime numbers?

....

Explain how you found your answer.

....

....

Mixed questions

1 **a** 1001 is the product of three different prime numbers.

What are they? ....

b 1001 has eight factors. Find them all.

....

2 Mia is doing a calculation. Here is her rule:

Choose a number ⟶ square it ⟶ add the first number ⟶ add 41

a Check the answers in this table.

b Fill in the rest of the table.

Number	Answer
1	$1^2 + 1 + 41 = 43$
2	$2^2 + 2 + 41 = 47$
3	$3^2 + 3 + 41 =$
4	
5	

c Mia says 'Start with any whole number. The answer is always a prime number.'

Is Mia correct? Give a reason for your answer.

....

....

....

....

....

3 16 is a square number.

a How does the diagram show that $1 + 3 + 5 + 7 = 16$?

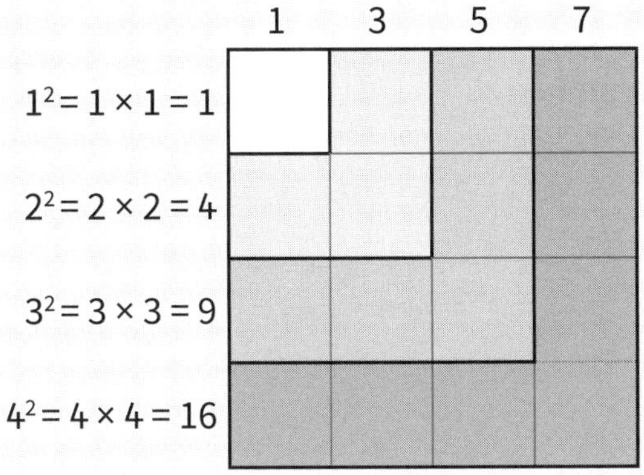

b Find results like this for other square numbers.

....

....

....

c Add up all the odd numbers less than 100.

$1 + 3 + 5 + 7 + \dots + 93 + 95 + 97 + 99 =$ ....

Explain a quick way to find the answer.

....

....

....

2 Sequences, expressions and formulae

2.1 Generating sequences (1)

1 Write down the next two terms of each sequence.

a 3.8, 4.1, 4.4, ..., ...

b 9.1, 8.7, 8.3, ..., ...

c 10, 4, −2, ..., ...

d −15, −13.5, −12, ..., ...

e $\frac{1}{2}, \frac{1}{4}, \frac{1}{8}$, ..., ...

f $\frac{1}{3}, \frac{2}{5}, \frac{3}{7}$, ..., ...

Look at the pattern of numbers in the numerators and denominators separately.

2 What is the term-to-term rule for this sequence?

2, 4, 10, 28, ...

3 Write down two different ways to continue each of these sequences.

Write down the term-to-term rule that you used and the next two numbers.

a 1, 5, ...

....

b 2, 7, ...

....

2.2 Generating sequences (2)

4 Look at these patterns made from squares.

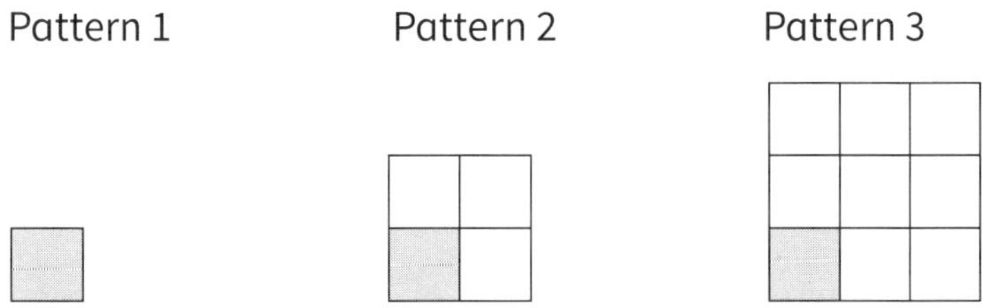

a How many small squares will there be in the fourth pattern? ......

b What is the name given to the number sequence formed by the total number of small squares in each pattern? ....

c How many grey squares will be in the following?

i the fifth pattern ....

ii the tenth pattern ....

d How many white squares will be in the following?

i the fifth pattern ....

ii the tenth pattern ....

2.3 Representing simple functions

1 In this two-step function machine, the input is 3 and the output is 16.

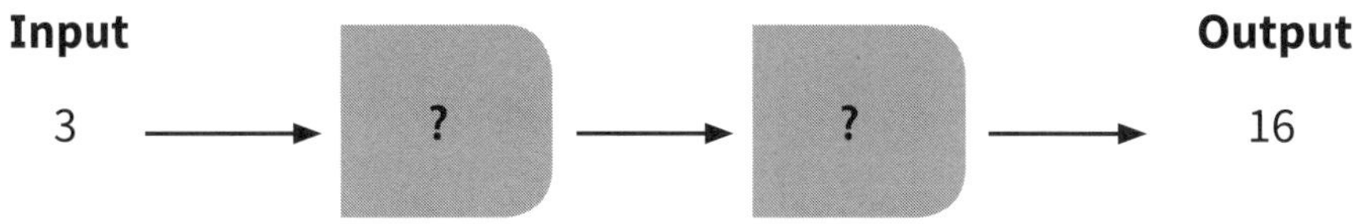

Write down three different two-step rules that this function machine could have.

....

....

....

2 This is part of Dakarai's homework. He has spilt tomato sauce on some of the numbers.

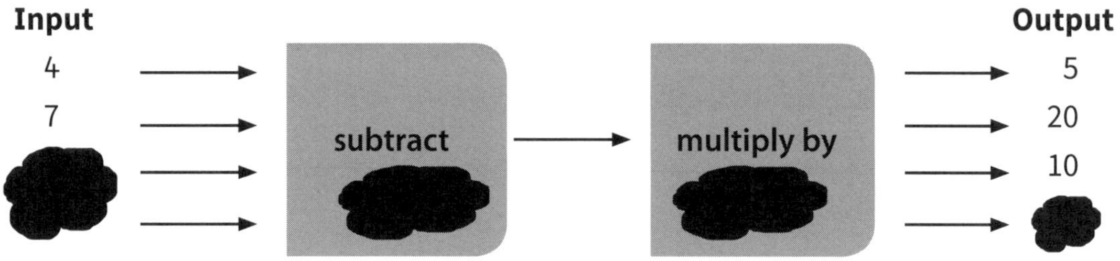

a Work out the numbers that are covered by tomato sauce.

....

....

....

b Is it possible to work out all the numbers? ....

If not, what numbers could the missing numbers be?

....

....

....

2.4 Constructing expressions

1 Write an algebraic expression for each of these.

a x more than y ....

b x less than y ....

c m more than two times n ....

d a less than three times b ....

e h multiplied by itself ....

f w divided by z ....

2 Write an algebraic expression for the output of each function machine.

You write $x \times 2$ as $2x$.

a x → ×2 → +3 → ....

b x → ×5 → −6 → ....

c x → +7 → ×4 → ....

You will need a bracket for the $(x + 7)$.

d x → ÷2 → +9 → ....

e x → −8 → ÷4 → ....

2.5 Deriving and using formulae

1 The weight of an object is calculated using the formula:

$$W = mg$$

where W = weight (in Newtons), m = mass (in kg) and g = acceleration due to gravity (in m/s^2).

On Earth $g = 10\,m/s^2$, while on the Moon $g = 1.6\,m/s^2$.

The mass of a man is 75 kg and the mass of a lunar landing module is 10 344 kg.

a Work out the weight of **i** the man and **ii** the lunar landing module on Earth.

i ....

ii ....

b Work out the weight of **i** the man and **ii** the lunar landing module on the Moon.

i ....

ii ....

2 The formula for converting a temperature in Farenheit (*F*) to Celsius (*C*) is:

$$C = \frac{5(F-32)}{9}$$

a Convert these temperatures into °C.

i 50 °F ....

ii −67 °F ....

b What temperature is the same in °F as it is in °C?

....

....

Mixed questions

1 Shen says that this function machine always gives outputs that are even numbers.

Input → $\times 2$ → $+4$ → Output

Is he correct? Explain your answer.

....

....

2 Look at this function machine.

Input ? → $\times 2$ → $+5$ → -5 → $\div 2$ → Output ?

a Try the function machine for three different whole number values.

....

....

....

b What do you notice about your answers to part a)? Why does this happen?

....

....

....

c Write your own four-step function machine that always gives you the same number that you started with.

3 A 'mind reader' says to you:

'Think of a number, then add three and double the result. Then subtract the number you first thought of, then subtract four, then finally subtract the number you first thought of again.'

a What answer do you get? ....

b Will you always get the same answer, whatever number you choose? ....

c Explain why this happens.

Write an expression to help you explain.

....

....

4 p and q are whole numbers such that $p + q = -2$ and $pq = -8$. Also $p > q$.

Work out the values of p and q.

....

....

....

3 Place value, ordering and rounding

3.1 Understanding decimals

1 Here is a secret code box.

																	Y	?
$\frac{7}{100}$	$\frac{2}{100}$	$\frac{3}{1000}$		$\frac{3}{10}$	$\frac{3}{1000}$	$\frac{7}{10}$	$\frac{5}{100}$	$\frac{7}{1000}$	$\frac{7}{100}$	$\frac{2}{1000}$	$\frac{3}{100}$		$\frac{3}{1000}$	$\frac{7}{100}$	$\frac{3}{100}$	$\frac{2}{10}$	

Look at the numbers in the box below. Work out the value of the underlined number, then find that number in the box above. Finally, write the letter that corresponds to the number in the secret code box.

The first one is done for you: $4.\underline{2}36$ → the value of the 2 is $\frac{2}{10}$, so the letter Y goes above $\frac{2}{10}$ in the table.

Y	$4.\underline{2}36$		R	$9.0\underline{2}4$		I	$6.1\underline{5}1$		A	$0.4\underline{7}5$		D	$6.\underline{3}1$
S	$18.0\underline{3}9$		M	$0.45\underline{7}$		L	$0.94\underline{2}$		C	$18.\underline{7}54$		E	$0.04\underline{3}$

3.2 Multiplying and dividing by 10, 100 and 1000

1 The formula to work out the area of a rectangular room is:

Area (square metres) = length (metres) × width (metres)

When Greg lays a floor he uses 10 screws per square metre.

How many screws does he need to lay a floor in a rectangular room that has a length of 5 m and a width of 3 m?

....

....

2 Brad lives in the USA. He goes on holiday to Kenya and then to Botswana.

Brad changes $1250 into Kenyan shillings (KES). While in Kenya he spends 63 520 KES.

He changes the rest of his Kenyan shillings into Botswanan Pula (BWP).

While in Botswana he spends 5725 BWP.

1$ = 100 KES   1 BWP = 10 KES

How many BWP does Brad have left at the end of his holiday?

....

....

....

....

3.3 Ordering decimals

1 Put the following in order of size, starting with the smallest.

2110 ÷ 100   0.0208 × 100   2320 ÷ 1000   2000 ÷ 1000   1.9 × 10   0.23 × 10

....

....

....

....

....

3.4 Rounding

1 George has rounded an integer to the nearest 10. His answer is 240.

a What is the smallest his integer could be? ....

b What is the largest his integer could be? ....

2 Lisa has rounded a number with three decimal places to one decimal place. Her answer is 8.7.

a What is the smallest her number could be? ....

b What is the largest her number could be? ....

3 **a** Use a calculator to work out the value of these square roots. Complete the table.

	Full calculator display	**Rounded to 1 decimal place**
$\sqrt{7}$		
$\sqrt{8}$		
$\sqrt{10}$		
$\sqrt{11}$		

b Explain why you think $\sqrt{9}$ was not included in the table.

....

....

....

....

4 The number 49 653 295 can be rounded in different ways.

To the nearest 1000 it is 49 653 000. To the nearest 100 000 it is 49 700 000.

Round the number 85 267 495 to the nearest:

a 1000 ....

b 10 000 ....

c 1 000 000 ....

d 10 000 000 ....

3.5 Adding and subtracting decimals

1 This is part of Evan's bank statement. It shows the money he pays into his bank account and the money he pays out of his bank account. The balance is the money left in his account after the amount has gone in or out.
Fill in the missing values.

Date	Item	Money in ($)	Money out ($)	Balance ($)
01/04				245.76
02/04	Wages	475.00		....
05/04	Groceries		67.50	....
07/04	Gas bill		134.28	....
11/04	Tax refund	65.30		....
15/04	Clothes		....	529.29

The balance on 02/04 is the balance on 01/04 plus his wages of $475.00.

3.6 Multiplying decimals

1 Use the fact that $0.43 \times 28 = 12.04$ to work out:

a $4.3 \times 28 =$ ....

b $43 \times 2.8 =$ ....

c $0.43 \times 280 =$ ....

d $0.043 \times 28 =$ ....

3.7 Dividing decimals

1 Shaun and four friends order a meal. The total cost of the meal is \$68.60.

Shaun orders: Chicken korma \$9.45, Pilau rice \$2.20 and Plain naan \$1.95.

Is Shaun better off if he pays for his own food rather than an equal share of the bill?

....

....

....

....

2 Use the fact that $47.7 \div 5.3 = 9$ to work out:

a $477 \div 5.3 =$ ....

b $47.7 \div 0.53 =$ ....

c $4.77 \div 0.53 =$ ....

d $4770 \div 5.3 =$ ....

3.8 Estimating and approximating

1 A surfboard hire shop uses this formula to work out the total cost, \$$C$, to hire a surfboard for d days:

$$C = 15d + 5$$

a Work out the cost of hiring a surfboard for one week.

....

b Check your answer to part a) using inverse operations.

....

2 A formula used to work out the final velocity, v, of an object is:

$v = u + at$ where: u is the starting velocity
a is the acceleration
t is the time

a ESTIMATE the value of v when $u = 8.8$, $a = 5.1$ and $t = 3$.

....

....

b CALCULATE the actual value of v when $u = 8.8$, $a = 5.1$ and $t = 3$.

....

....

c Was your answer to part a) a good estimate of the actual value?

....

Mixed questions

1 Here are some formula cards.

$B = 3E - A$	$E = 2A$	$C = E - 5.22$	$D = F \div 4$
$G = F \div C$	$F = 10C$		$H = (D + F) \div G$

a Work out the value of H when $A = 4.2$.

Write down the order in which you used the cards.

....

....

....

....

....

....

....

....

b Which formula do you NOT need in order to work out H?

....

c Write your own formula that connects A to H.

....

....

4.1 Knowing metric units

1 Complete these addition pyramids. Each brick is the sum of the two bricks below it.

a

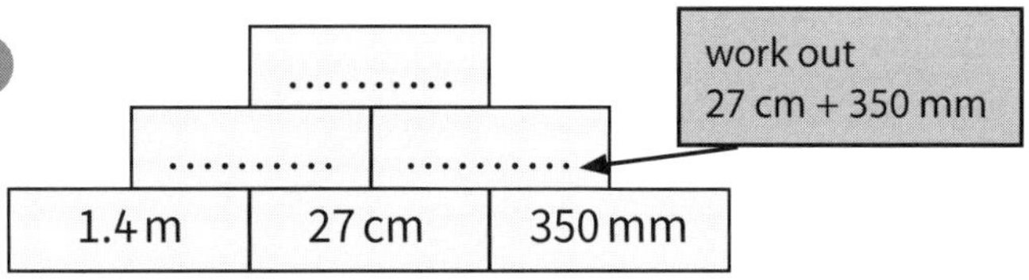

It is up to you what units you use, but make sure you use the same units when adding.

b

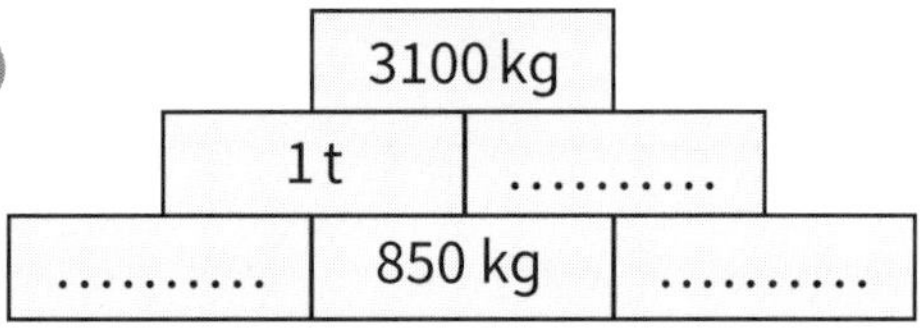

2 The diagram shows three containers. The biggest container is full of water.

Using only these containers, how can you end up with the following amounts in the largest container?

a 3 l ....

b 2750 ml ....

c 4.5 l ....

3 100 silver bracelets weigh 62 kg. The value of silver is $0.52 per gram.

What is the value of the silver in one bracelet?

....

....

4.2 Choosing suitable units

1 Here is a secret code box.

							N			
1 litre	190 kg	250 ml	80 litres		340 g	420 g	590 kg		1200 kg	42 km

							!
	1 litre	40 075 km	250 ml	340 g	46 g	6853 km	!

Look at the statements in the box below. Decide which of the numbers from the secret code box correctly completes each statement. Finally, write the letter that corresponds to that number in the secret code box.

The first one has been done for you.

N	The average mass of an African buffalo is 590 kg
T	The amount of fruit juice in a carton is ....
E	The length of a marathon is about ....
I	The amount of cola in a small bottle is ....
A	The average mass of a football is ....
R	The length of the equator is ....
H	The average mass of a male lion is ....
B	The average mass of a male giraffe is ....
S	The average amount of water used in a bath is ....
Y	The length of the Nile river is ....
K	The average mass of a golf ball is ....
C	The amount of honey in a regular jar is ....

4.3 Reading scales

1 The diagram shows two thermometers.

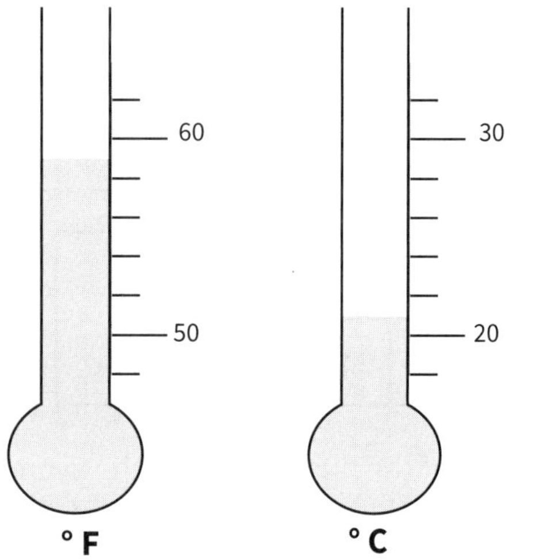

The formula to convert degrees Fahrenheit (F) into degrees Celsius (C) is:

$$C = \frac{5}{9}(F - 32)$$

What is the difference in the temperatures shown?

....

2 Carole puts a full cup of water into the jug. It fills it to the level shown.

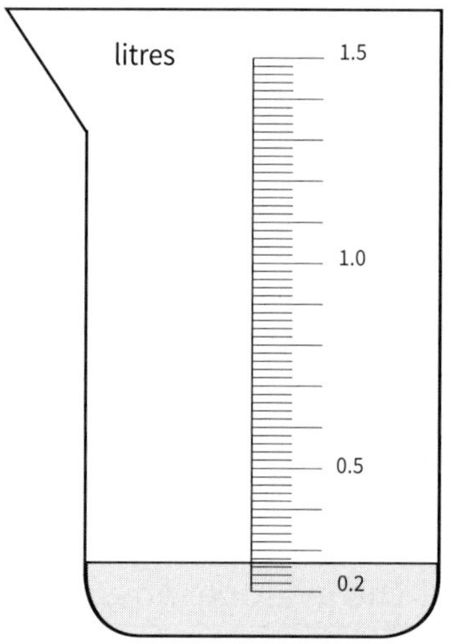

a How much more water is needed to fill the jug to the 1.5 litre level?

....

....

b How many more full cups are needed to do this?

....

....

3 Adi cuts a piece of wood into three smaller pieces of equal length.

The scale shows the length of one of the smaller pieces.

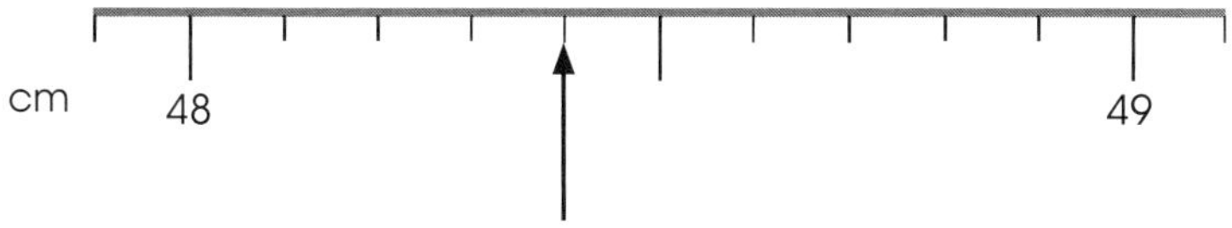

How long was the piece of wood Adi started with? Give your answer in metres.

....

Mixed questions

1 The measuring jug shown contains honey. 1 litre of honey has a mass of 1.4 kg.

a What is the mass of the honey in the jug? ....

....

b A full jar of honey contains 425 g. Harsha pours the honey from the jug into an empty jar.

How many more millilitres of honey does she need to add to the jar to fill it?

....

....

....

2 In some countries distances are measured in miles, in others distances are measured in kilometres. The connection between miles and kilometres is:

1 mile ≈ 1.6 km

The symbol ≈ means 'is approximately equal to'.

Karen drives from her home to work.

a On her way to work Karen passes a road sign that shows a speed limit of 50 miles per hour. How fast is this in kilometres per hour?

....

....

b These are the mileage readings on Karen's car odometer before and after her journey.

30 986	**31 006**
before	after

The odometer shows the total number of miles the car has travelled.

How far, in kilometres, is it from Karen's home to her work?

....

c The journey takes Karen 40 minutes. She uses this formula to work out her average speed:

$$\text{Average speed in km per hour} = \frac{\text{distance in km}}{\text{time in minutes}} \times 60$$

What is Karen's average speed for her journey to work?

....

....

5.1 Drawing and measuring angles

1 This diagram shows two acute angles put together to make an obtuse angle.

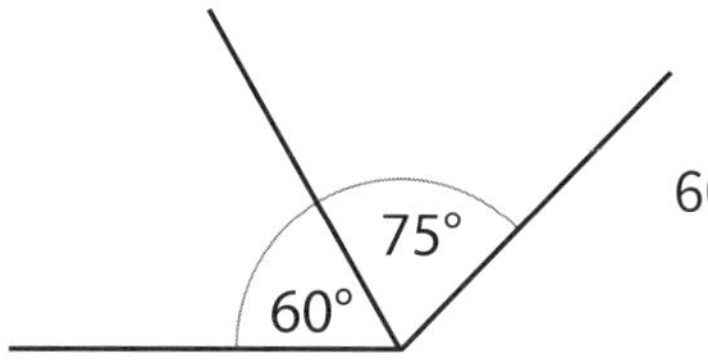

$60° + 75° = 135°$

Write down whether the following are possible or not. Either give an example or explain why each is not possible.

a Two acute angles put together to make an acute angle.

b An obtuse angle and an acute angle put together to make a reflex angle.

c Two obtuse angles put together to make an obtuse angle.

2 Look at this triangle:

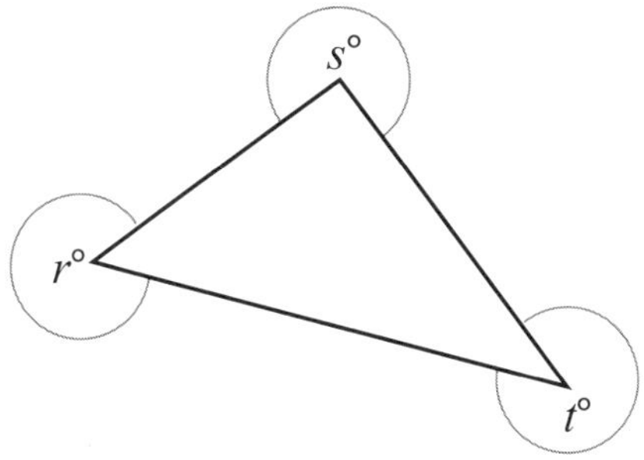

Explain why $r + s + t$ must equal 900.

....

....

....

....

5.2 Calculating angles

1 **a** One angle of an isosceles triangle is 110°.

Work out the other two angles. ....

b One angle of an isosceles triangle is 50°.

Work out the other two angles. ....

c There is more than one answer to part b). Did you find them both?

Explain why there is one answer to part a) but more than one to part b).

....

....

2 A quadrilateral has four angles.

Look at the following statements. Write down whether each statement COULD be true or MUST be false. Give a reason for your answer.

a A quadrilateral has four acute angles.

....

....

b A quadrilateral has two acute angles and two obtuse angles.

....

....

c A quadrilateral has four obtuse angles.

....

....

Mixed questions

1 Five identical isosceles triangles are put together to make a five-sided shape.

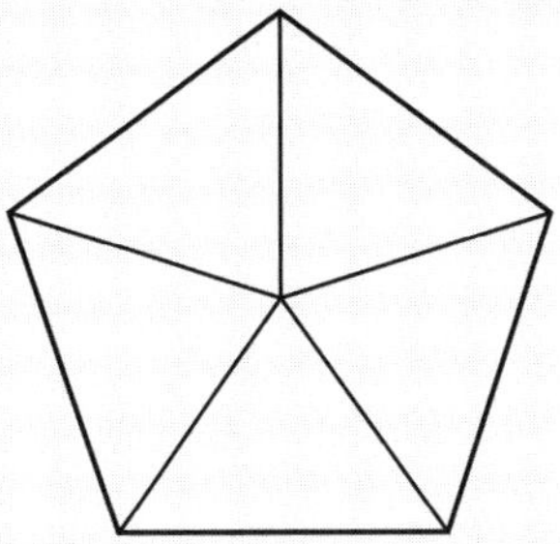

Work out the angles of each triangle.

....

....

2 Eight identical isosceles triangles are put together to make an eight-sided shape.

a Sketch the shape.

b Work out the angles of each isosceles triangle.

....

....

3 The largest angle of a triangle is three times the size of the smallest angle.

The other angle is twice the size of the smallest one.

Find the angles of the triangle.

....

....

4 The corners of three squares are joined to make this shape.

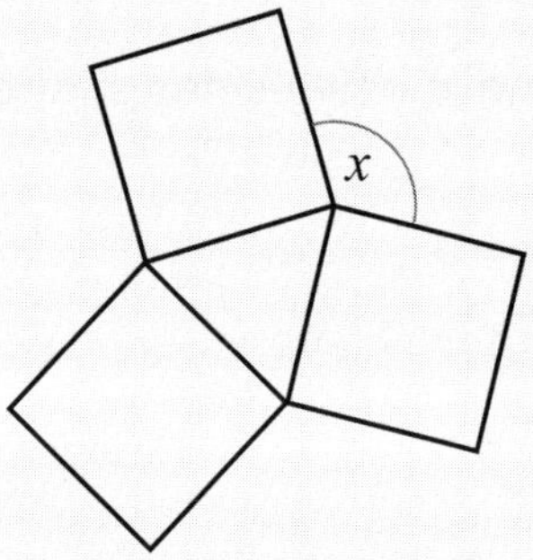

Work out the size of the angle marked x.

....

....

5 This six-sided shape is divided into two quadrilaterals.

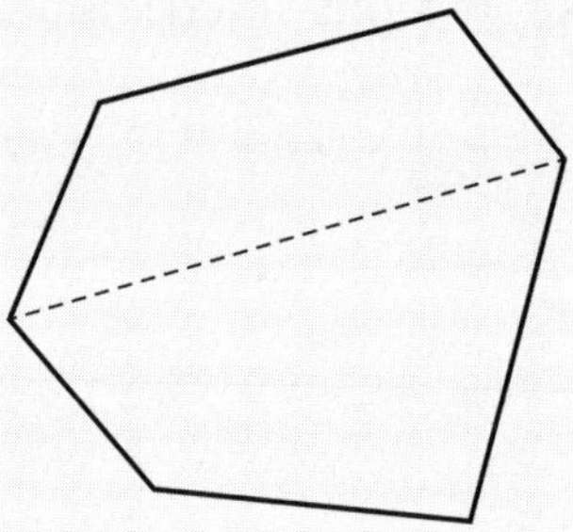

a What can you say about the sum of the angles of the six-sided shape?

Give a reason for your answer.

....

....

b Is your answer to part a) true for ANY six-sided shape?

Give a reason for your answer.

....

....

6 Planning and collecting data

6.1 Planning to collect data

1 Jake wants to find out the favourite subjects of students in his school.

He asks all the members of the school maths club.

Odita says: 'That will not give a fair result.'

a Explain why Odita is correct.

....

....

....

....

b Explain how Jake should collect the data he needs.

....

....

....

....

2 Describe different ways in which you could collect data to answer this question:

'Do people prefer to use Facebook or Twitter?'

....

....

....

....

....

....

6.2 Collecting data

1 Design a questionnaire that could be used in your school to find out students' views on school uniform.

You must ask at least three questions.

Make sure you include response sections in your questionnaire.

....

....

....

....

....

....

....

....

....

....

....

6.3 Using frequency tables

1 Mr Patel gives his class a mental maths test. These are the students' scores out of 25:

23	20	18	15	9	12	6	17	5
24	21	6	9	11	24	4	25	18
10	18	21	7	22	13	2		

a **i** Complete this grouped frequency table.

Score	Tally	Frequency
1–18		
19–25		
	Total	

ii Emyr says that this is not a good way of showing the data.

Is Emyr correct? Explain your answer.

....

....

b Draw a better grouped frequency table for the data.

2 Ada records the time it takes the students in her class to complete a magic square.

These are the times, in seconds:

26.0	21.4	25.5	27.4	24.9	32.9	18.9	15.0	32.4	29.3
34.5	29.1	27.2	33.3	28.8	31.5	26.8	34.8	22.9	16.1
17.5	23.5	30.0	14.3	25.0	24.8	29.1	10.1	25.8	18.4

Complete the grouped frequency table below for this data.

The group $10 \le t < 15$ includes the values from 10 up to, but not including, 15.

The group $15 \le t < 20$ includes the values from 15 up to, but not including, 20.

Time (t seconds)	Tally	Frequency
$10 \le t < 15$		
$15 \le t < 20$		
$20 \le t < 25$		
$25 \le t < 30$		
$30 \le t < 35$		
	Total	

Mixed questions

1 A calculator has a random number generator button (Ran#).

When you press this button, the calculator gives you a random decimal number between 0 and 1.

a Using your calculator, work out 100 × Ran# and write down the number you get.

....

b Repeat part a) ten times and write down all the numbers you get.

....

....

c Design a grouped frequency table to record the numbers you get when you work out 100 × Ran#.

d Work out 100 × Ran# 50 times. Record the data on your grouped frequency table.

e Look at the results in your table for part d).

Do you think your calculator is choosing numbers at random? Explain your answer.

....

....

....

....

7 Fractions

7.1 Simplifying fractions

1 **a** What fraction of this shape is shaded?

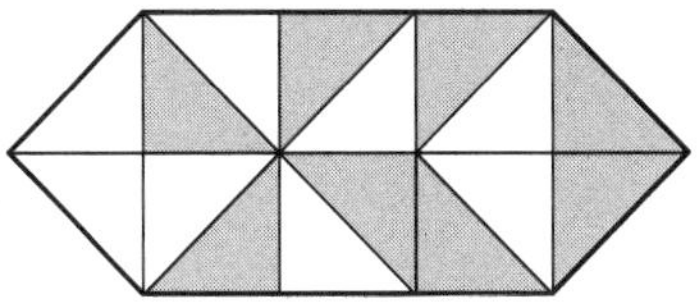

....

b How many more triangles must be shaded so that $\frac{5}{8}$ of the shape is shaded?

....

2 Write each of these as a fraction of an hour in its simplest form.

> 15 minutes as a fraction of an hour is $\frac{15}{60} = \frac{?}{?}$

a 15 minutes ......

b 12 minutes ......

c 20 minutes ......

d 42 minutes ......

e 55 minutes ......

3 Which of these fractions is the odd one out? Explain how you made your decision.

$\frac{54}{126}$ $\frac{36}{84}$ $\frac{48}{80}$ $\frac{45}{105}$

....

....

....

7.2 Recognising equivalent fractions, decimals and percentages

1 In a 20 g piece of iron ore, 14 g is actually iron.

a Write the amount of iron in the iron ore as:

i a fraction .... **ii** a percentage ....

b What percentage of the iron ore is NOT iron? Show your working.

....

2 A recipe uses 1 kg of flour. Of that, 300 g is rice flour and 0.25 kg is rye flour.

a What **i** fraction and **ii** percentage of the total amount of flour is rice flour?

i .... **ii** ....

b What **i** fraction and **ii** percentage of the total amount of flour is rye flour?

i .... **ii** ....

7.3 Comparing fractions

1 **a** Complete these equivalent fractions.

$\frac{2}{3} = \frac{}{18}$ $\frac{4}{9} = \frac{}{18}$ $\frac{5}{6} = \frac{}{18}$

b Write the fractions $\frac{2}{3}$, $\frac{4}{9}$ and $\frac{5}{6}$ in order of size, starting with the smallest.

....

c Write the fractions $\frac{7}{12}$, $\frac{5}{6}$ and $\frac{3}{4}$ in order of size, starting with the smallest.

....

7.4 Improper fractions and mixed numbers

1 Write each of the following times as a mixed number in its simplest form.

a 1 hour 15 minutes ....

b 3 hours 20 minutes ....

c 2 hours 10 minutes ....

2 Write these improper fractions as decimals.

a $\frac{16}{5}$ ....

b $\frac{11}{4}$ ....

c $\frac{18}{8}$ ....

Write the fraction as a mixed number first, then convert the fraction part to a decimal.

3 Write these decimals as improper fractions.

a 5.5 ....

b 3.6 ....

c 1.25 ....

7.5 Adding and subtracting fractions

1 Work out these additions. Write each answer in its simplest form.

a $1\frac{3}{8} + 4\frac{1}{2}$ ....

b $1\frac{3}{8} + 1\frac{3}{4}$ ....

c $1\frac{3}{8} + 6\frac{2}{3}$ ....

2 Work out these subtractions. Write each answer in its simplest form.

a $\frac{3}{4} - \frac{3}{7}$ ....

b $\frac{1}{3} - \frac{1}{4}$ ....

c $\frac{11}{12} - \frac{3}{8}$ ....

3 Work out these subtractions. Write each answer in its simplest form.

a $1\frac{1}{4} - \frac{5}{8}$ ....

b $3\frac{2}{5} - \frac{7}{10}$ ....

c $2\frac{1}{2} - \frac{2}{3}$ ....

7.6 Finding fractions of a quantity

1 This diagram shows the petrol gauge of a truck.

The petrol tank holds 176 litres when full.
How much petrol is in the tank?

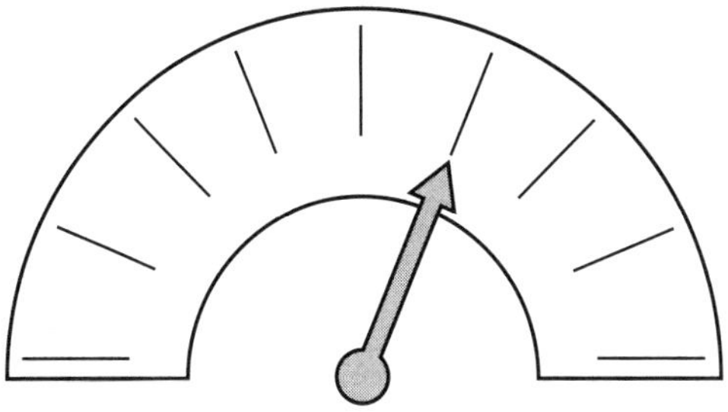

....

....

....

2 Lynn and Sal go on holiday.

Lynn takes \$500 and spends $\frac{3}{5}$ of her money.

Sal takes \$450 and spends $\frac{2}{3}$ of her money.

Who has the most money left at the end of the holiday?

....

....

....

7.7 Finding remainders

1 Each number in a rectangle is divided by a number in a circle, leaving the remainder in one of the triangles. Draw lines matching each rectangle to its circle and triangle.

100	179	137	213
÷ 8	÷ 6	÷ 7	÷ 9
R1	R2	R3	R8

Mixed questions

1 Using only the numbers from the numerator box and the denominator box, make three pairs of equivalent fractions. You must use all the numbers from both boxes.

Numerator box
1 2 3 3 6 8

Denominator box
2 3 4 6 8 12

—— and ——

—— and ——

—— and ——

2 John works out that $4\frac{1}{4} - 2\frac{3}{5} = 1\frac{13}{20}$

Is John correct? Show your working.

....

....

....

....

8 Symmetry

8.1 Recognising and describing 2D shapes and solids

1 Put each shape through this classification flow chart. Write down the letter where each shape comes out.

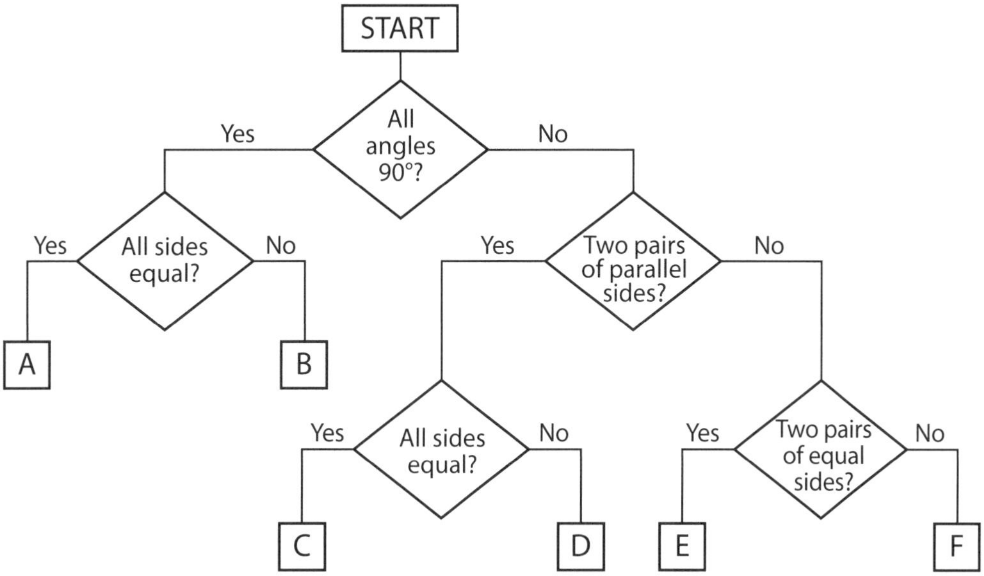

a parallelogram ....

b trapezium ....

c kite ....

d rectangle ....

e square ....

f rhombus ....

8.2 Recognising line symmetry

1 This cuboid has three planes of symmetry.
The first one is drawn and shaded for you.

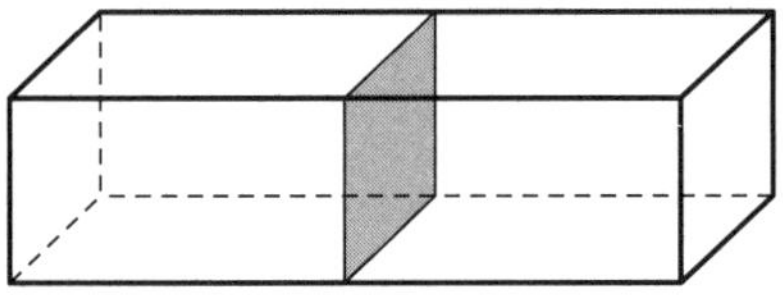

On the two diagrams of the same cuboid below, draw and shade in the other two planes of symmetry.

2 This triangular prism has two planes of symmetry.

On the two diagrams, draw and shade in the planes of symmetry.

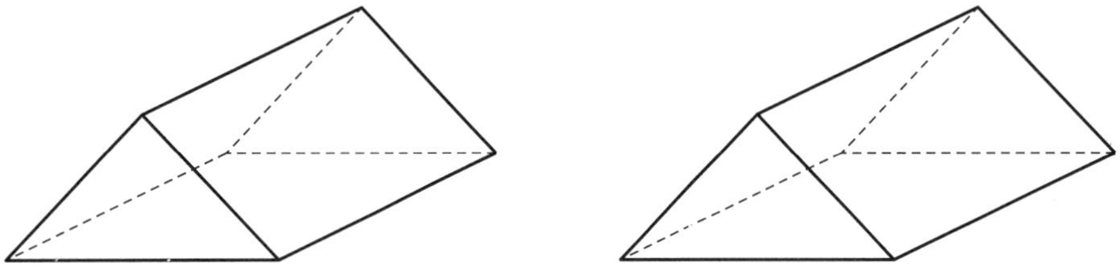

8.3 Recognising rotational symmetry

1 In each of these diagrams, shade two more triangles to make the shapes have the given order of rotational symmetry.

a Order 1

b Order 2

c Order 3

d Order 6

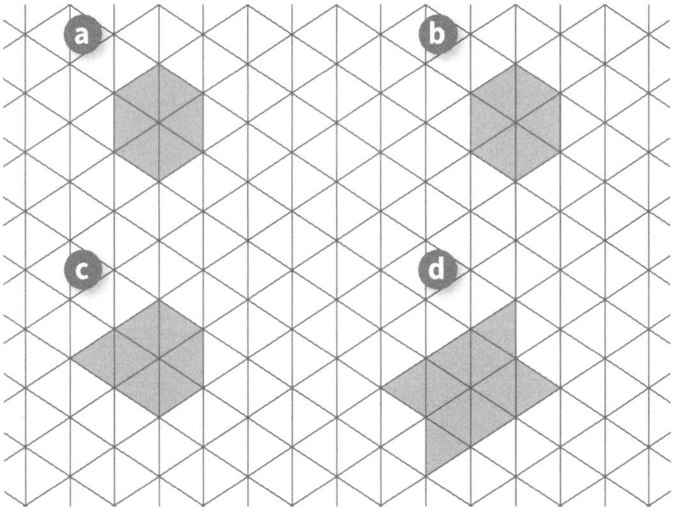

2 On the isometric paper, draw shapes that have rotational symmetry of:

a Order 1

b Order 2

c Order 3

Draw different shapes from those in Question 1.

8.4 Symmetry properties of triangles, special quadrilaterals and polygons

1 On the squared paper draw:

a a pentagon with one line of symmetry

b a hexagon with order 2 rotational symmetry

The shapes are not regular.

Mixed questions

1 A is the point (4, 7) and B is the point (6, 4). Plot both of these points on the two grids below.

a Plot two more points on the grid and join all four points to make a kite.

b Plot two more points on the grid and join all four points to make a trapezium.

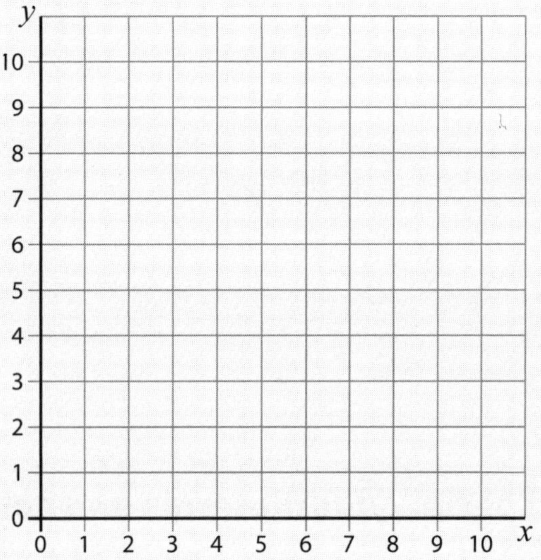

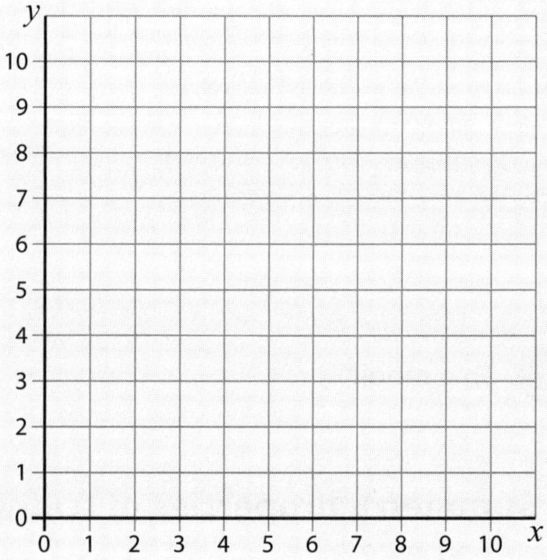

2 Look at Question 1 in Section 8.1 of this workbook.

Draw your own flow diagram to classify the following solid shapes.

a cube

b cuboid

c square-based pyramid

d cylinder

e cone

f triangular-based pyramid

g sphere

h triangular prism

9 Expressions and equations

9.1 Collecting like terms

1 Draw a line joining each rectangular card to its equivalent oval card.

Rectangular cards: $5x - 3x$ | $\frac{8x}{2}$ | $x \times x$ | $7x - 4x$ | $3 \times 3x$ | $5x \times x$ | $3x \times 2x$

Oval cards: $4x$ | $2x$ | $9x$ | $5x^2$ | x^2 | $3x$ | $6x^2$

2 In a magic square, the rows, columns and diagonals all add up to the same number.

a Write the numbers 1 to 9 in this magic square so that all the rows, columns and diagonals add up to 15.

You can use each number only once. Three numbers have been written in for you.

8		
	5	
	9	

b Write the algebraic expressions from the cloud in the magic square so that all the rows, columns and diagonals add up to $3b$.

$b - c$ $b - a - c$ $a + b - c$ $b + c$ $b - a$ $b + c - a$

$a + b$		
	b	
	$a + b + c$	

9.2 Expanding brackets

1 Expand and simplify these expressions.

a $3(x + 2) + 4x$ ....

b $4(9 + x) - 24$ ....

c $5(2x - 2) + x + 17$ ....

d $6(3x - 4) - 8x + 4$ ....

e $4(x + 4) + 7(x + 1)$ ....

f $8(5 + 2x) + 3(x - 6)$ ....

2 Show that $4(2x + 7) + 3(6x - 5) \equiv 13(2x + 1)$

'≡' means 'is equivalent to' or 'the same as'.

....

....

....

3 Work out the missing numbers in these expansions.

a $9(3x + 2) = 3(\square x + \square)$

....

....

b $5(8 - 6z) = 10(\square - \square z)$

....

....

9.3 Constructing and solving equations

1 For each of these diagrams:

i Write an equation involving the angles.

ii Solve your equation to find the value of x.

iii Work out the sizes of the angles in the diagram.

iv Check that your answers are correct.

Start with $x + x + 70° = 180°$.

a

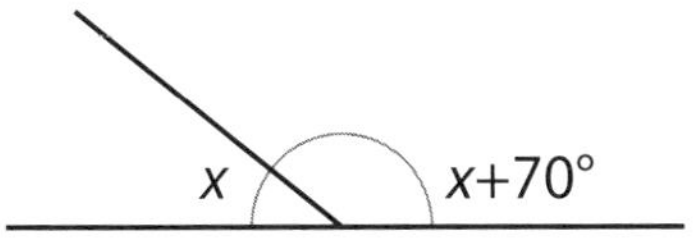

....

....

....

....

b

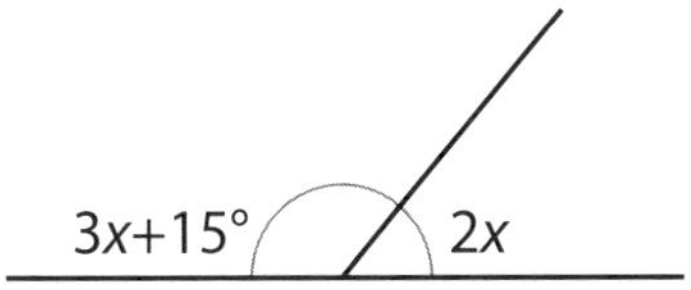

....

....

....

....

c

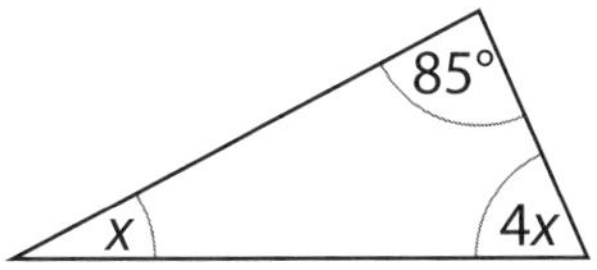

....

....

....

....

d

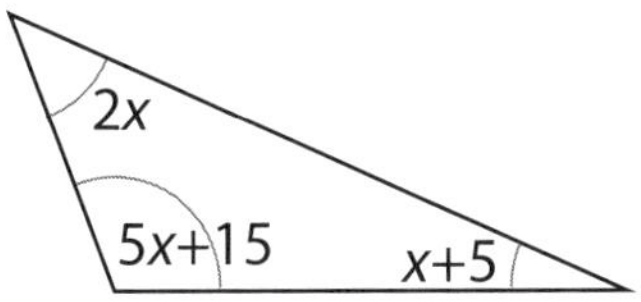

....

....

....

....

....

Mixed questions

1 For each of these diagrams:

i Write an equation involving the angles.

ii Solve your equation to find the value of x.

iii Work out the sizes of the angles in the diagram.

iv Check that your answers are correct.

a

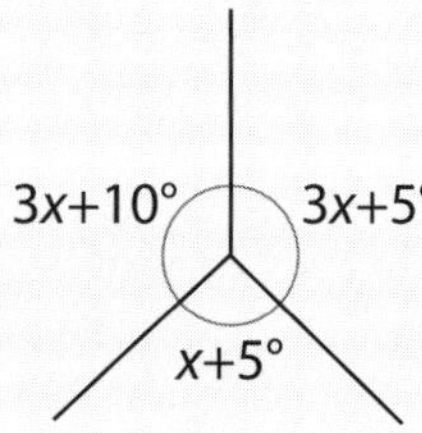

....

....

....

....

b

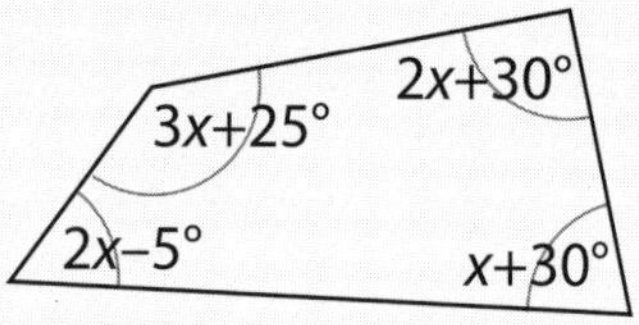

....

....

....

....

c

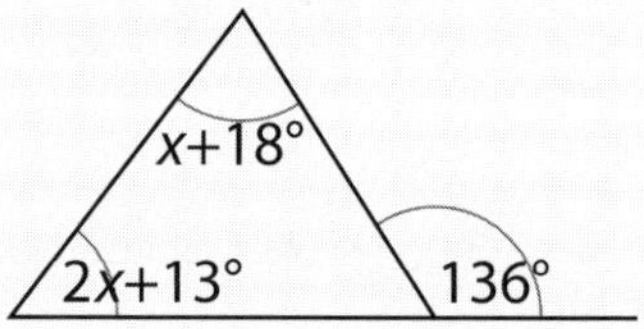

....

....

....

....

2 Solve these equations. Two of them have been started for you.

a $2(x + 5) = 24$

$2x + 10 = 24$

....

....

b $3(3x - 4) = 24$

....

....

c $\frac{x+2}{9} = 3$

$x + 2 = 3 \times 9$

....

....

d $\frac{2x-5}{8} = 2$

....

....

3 Write an equation for each of the statements below.

Solve the equation to find the value of the unknown number.

a I think of a number, add 6, and multiply the result by 5. The answer is 70.

....

....

....

....

b I think of a number, subtract 8 and divide the result by 3. The answer is 12.

....

....

....

....

10 Averages

10.1 Median, mode and range

1 The range of ages of a group of people is 29 years.

One person in the group is 35 years old. Another person in the group is 53 years old.

What is the youngest possible age of a person in the group?

...... years old

2 **a** Write down four numbers with a median of 20 and a range of 8.

....

b Write down four numbers with a mode of 22 and a range of 8.

....

c Write down four numbers with a median of 20, a mode of 22 and a range of 8.

....

3 Here is a list of eight numbers:

32 44 33 30 35 39 48 31 ......

Add one more number to the list to make the median 33 and the range 30.

4 The median height of a group of children is 120 cm.

The range of the heights is 25 cm.

One child is 145 cm tall.

What can you say about the heights of the other four children?

....

....

5 Here is a list of six test marks:

22 23 25 28 34 40

a Four of the marks are increased by two. The median does not change.

Which four marks are increased?

....

....

b Four of the marks are increased by two. The range does not change.

Which marks are increased? Give all possible answers.

....

....

6 A men's football team has a median mass of 70 kg and a range of 10 kg.

A women's football team has a median mass of 50 kg and a range of 8 kg.

a What is the smallest possible range for the two teams together? ...... kg

b What is the largest possible range for the two teams together? ...... kg

10.2 The mean

1 **a** Calculate the mean of each of these sets of numbers.

i 4 8 9 13 16 ......

ii 14 18 19 23 26 ......

iii 74 78 79 83 86 ......

iv 0 14 15 19 22 ......

b Without using a calculator, write down the mean of:

2134, 2138, 2139, 2143 and 2146

....

c A football team has played ten matches. The mean number of goals per match is 1.9.

How many goals must the team score in the next match to increase the mean to 2?

....

2 Here is a list of six numbers:

6 8 10 12 14 16

a Xavier removes one number. The mean of the remaining numbers is 10.4.

Which number did Xavier remove? ......

b Mia removes another number. The mean of the remaining numbers is now 11.5.

Which number did Mia remove? ......

3 There are 11 people in a football team.

The mean age of ten of the players is 20 years.

a If the mean age of the whole team is 21 years, how old is the eleventh person? ......

b Explain why it is very unlikely that the mean age for the team would be 25 years.

....

....

4 The mean distance travelled to work by 60 men is 12.5 km.

The mean distance travelled to work by 40 women is 8.4 km.

Work out the mean distance travelled by all 100 people.

....

5 This bar chart shows the number of brothers that 80 children have.

Work out the mean number of brothers.

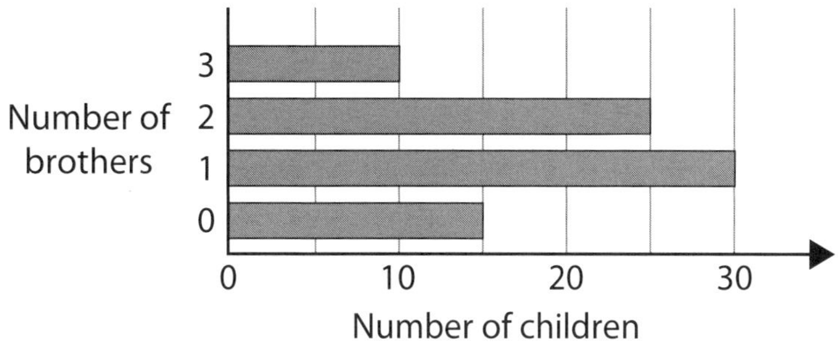

....

Mixed questions

1 Four numbers have a mode of 3, a median of 4 and a mean of 5.

Work out the range.

....

2 The mean wage of the people in an office is \$25 000 a year.

One person gets a pay rise of \$2000.

Tick (✓) to show whether these statements must be true, must be false or could be true or false.

	Must be true	Must be false	Could be true or false
The mean wage has increased.			
The median wage has increased.			
The range has increased.			
The range has decreased.			

3 Look at this list of numbers:

1 2 2 3 3 3 4 4 4 4 5 5 5 5 5

Find how many numbers are:

a less than the median ......

b greater than the median ......

c less than the mode ......

d greater than the mode ......

e less than the mean ......

f greater than the mean ......

4 Find five numbers where:

a the mode is less than the median AND the median is less than the mean

....

b the mode is less than the mean AND the mean is less than the median

....

c the mean is less than the mode AND the mode is less than the median

....

d the mean is less than the median AND the median is less than the mode.

....

5 Anders and Sasha each have a bag of coins.

The mean value of the coins in Anders' bag is 6 cents.

The mean value of the coins in Sasha's bag is 4 cents.

Anders takes a five cent coin out of his bag and gives it to Sasha.

What, if anything, can you say about the change in:

a the median value of the coins in Sasha's bag

....

b the range of values of the coins in Sasha's bag

....

c the mean value of the coins in Sasha's bag?

....

11 Percentages

11.1 Simple percentages

1 Write down these fractions as percentages.

a $\frac{1}{2}$ = ...

b $\frac{1}{4}$ = ...

c $\frac{1}{8}$ = ...

d $\frac{1}{16}$ = ...

2 Write down these fractions as percentages.

a $\frac{1}{8}$ = ...

b $\frac{3}{8}$ = ...

c $\frac{5}{8}$ = ...

d $\frac{7}{8}$ = ...

3 Look at this fact: 5% = $\frac{1}{20}$

Use it to help you write the following as fractions.

a 15% = ...

b 2.5% = ...

c 45% = ...

d 7.5% = ...

4 Percentages can be greater than 100%:

150% = $1\frac{1}{2}$ 200% = 2 225% = $2\frac{1}{4}$

Write each of the following as a percentage.

a $1\frac{1}{4}$ = ...

b $1\frac{3}{4}$ = ...

c $2\frac{1}{2}$ = ...

d $1\frac{3}{10}$ = ...

5 Write these as mixed numbers.

a 110% = ... b 180% = ...

c 230% = ... d 105% = ...

6 Complete the table.

Percentage	20%	40%	65%	130%	175%	190%
Fraction						
Decimal		0.4				

7 Here are some statements. Circle to show if each one is possible or impossible.

a The population of a city increased by 120%. possible impossible

b The price of a car was reduced by 120%. possible impossible

c The footballer said: 'My effort was 120%.' possible impossible

d My tree is 120% taller than yours. possible impossible

11.2 Calculating percentages

1 17.5% = 10% + 5% + 2.5%

Use this fact to work out 17.5% of:

a $80 ...... b $64 ......

c $450 ...... d $36 ......

2 Work out these percentages of \$4200.

a 10% ......

b 0.5% ......

c 3.5%......

d 49.5% ......

3 Work out these percentages of 72 kg.

a 12.5% ......

b 37.5% ......

c 62.5%......

d 87.5% ......

4 This is how Shen finds 45% of \$2400:

10% = \$240 5% = \$120 45% = 4 × 240 + 120 = \$1080.

Find a shorter method. Show that it gives the same answer.

....

....

5 Work out:

a 30% of 60 kg = ...

b 130% of 60 kg = ...

c 230% of 60 kg = ...

6 Work out:

a 10% of \$53 = ...

b 53% of \$10 = ...

c 45% of 30 kg = ...

d 30% of 45 kg = ...

e 5% of 120 km = ...

f 120% of 5 km = ...

7 Look at your answers to Question 6. Describe what you see. Is this always true?

....

....

8 Work out:

a 15% of \$4300 = ... **b** 1.5 % of \$4300 = ... **c** 150% of \$4300 = ...

9 3.8% of \$270 = \$10.26

Use this fact to work out:

a 4.8% of \$270 = ... **b** 2.8% of \$270 = ... **c** 7.6% of \$270 = ...

10 87% of \$690 = \$600.30

Use this fact to work out:

a 8.7% of \$690 = ... **b** 97% of \$690 = ... **c** 187% of \$690 = ...

Mixed questions

1 Which is larger, 7.5% of \$6100 or 21% of \$2200?

....

2 Fill in the missing numbers:

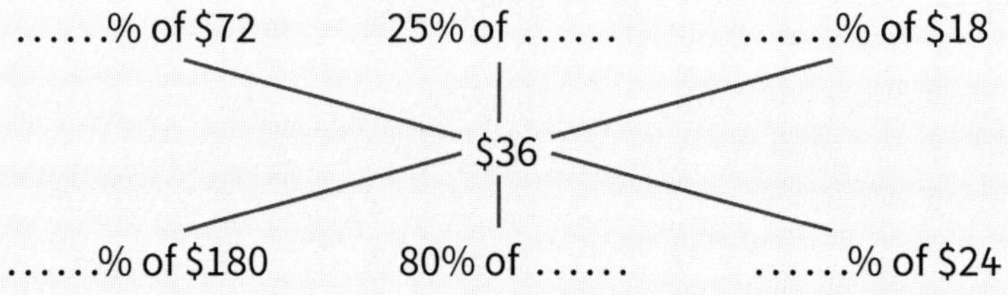

3 Fill in the missing numbers.

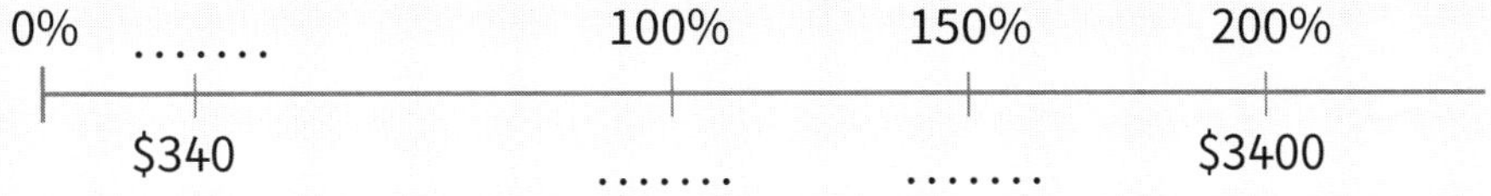

4 The height of a plant in March is 30 cm.

The height of the plant in June is 42 cm.

a Work out the increase in height.

....

Complete these sentences:

b The height in June is ......% more than the height in March.

c The height in June is ......% of the height in March.

5 The population of a town in 1985 was 60 000.

The population of the town in 2000 was 20% higher.

a Work out the population in 2000.

....

b The population in 2015 was 20% lower than the population in 2000.

Tanesha says: 'The population in 2015 must be 60 000.'

Show that Tanesha is NOT correct.

....

....

12 Constructions

12.1 Measuring and drawing lines

1 What is the total length of this line? Explain how you worked out your answer.

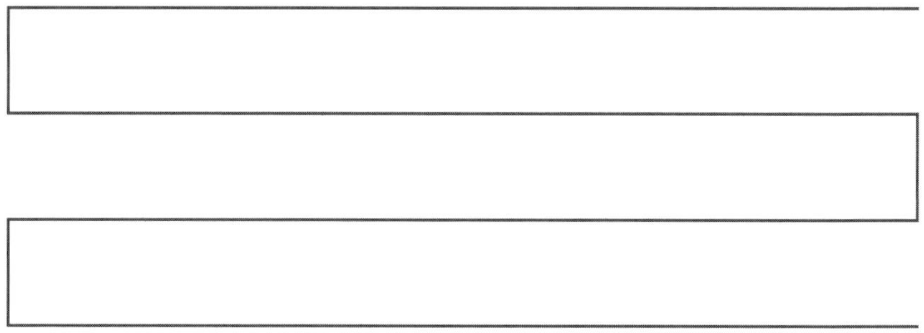

....

....

2 **a** Use a ruler to draw straight lines along the length of this curve. Measure the lines and work out the total, to estimate the length of the curve.

The first two lines have been drawn for you.

b Lay a piece of string along the length of the curve, then measure the length of the string with a ruler. Write down your answer.

....

....

c Do you think your answer to part a) or b) is the most accurate measurement of the length of the curve? Explain your answer.

....

....

12.2 Drawing perpendicular and parallel lines

1 **a** Draw an accurate copy of this diagram.

AB = 4 cm
BC = 2 cm
BE = 3 cm
DE = 3 cm
EF = 4 cm
FG = 1 cm
FH = 3 cm

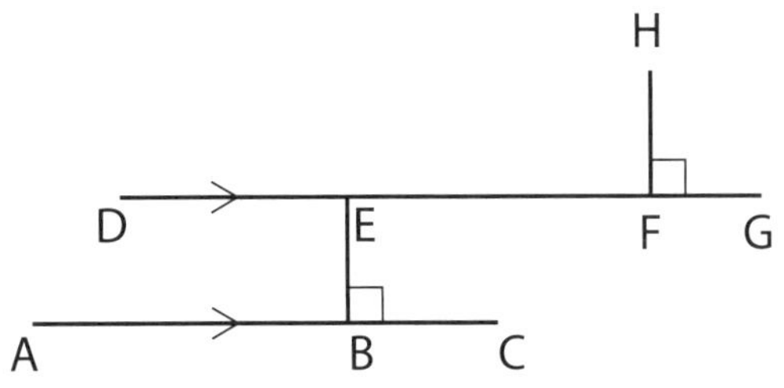

b Draw and measure the line AD and the line CH. ....

c Are AD and CH parallel? Explain your answer.

....

....

12.3 Constructing triangles

1 Draw an accurate copy of this parallelogram.

Use your knowledge of how to construct a triangle to do this.

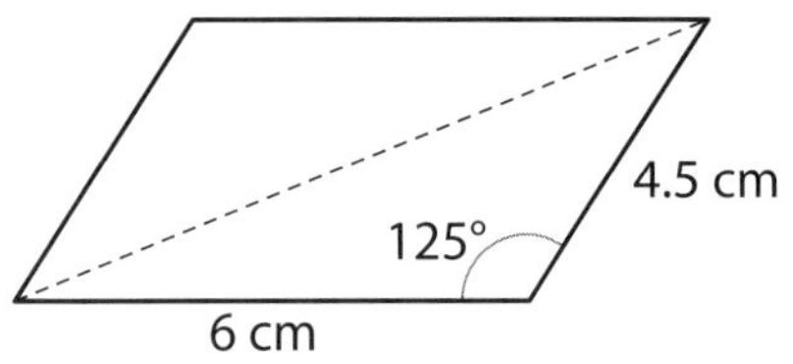

12.4 Constructing squares, rectangles and polygons

1 **a** Draw an accurate copy of this irregular pentagon.

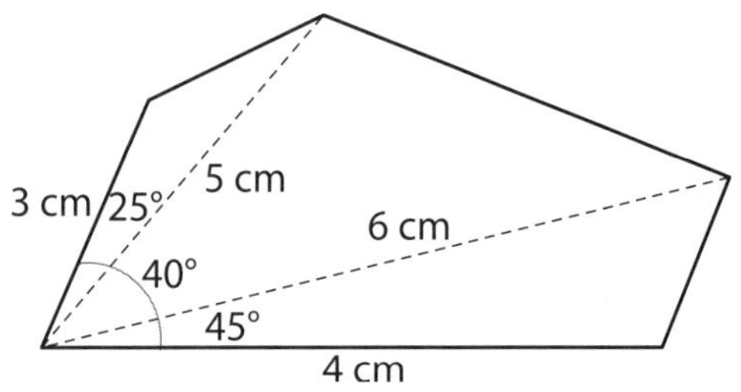

b Measure all the interior angles in your pentagon in part a). Write the angles in the pentagon below.

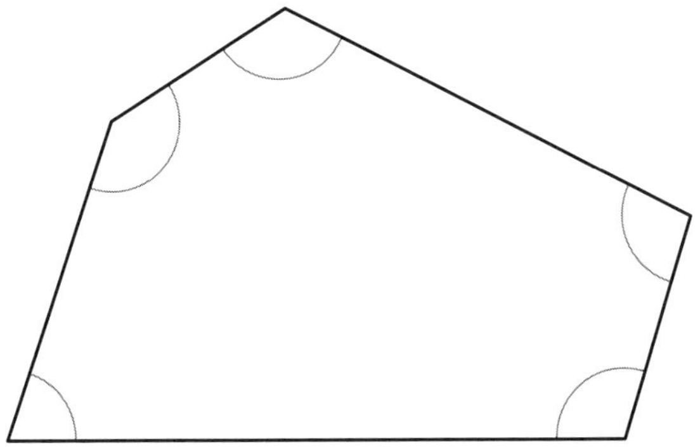

What is the total of all the angles?

....

....

Do you think your drawing is accurate? Explain your answer using the total of all the angles above.

....

....

....

Mixed questions

1 The sketch shows the side of a house.

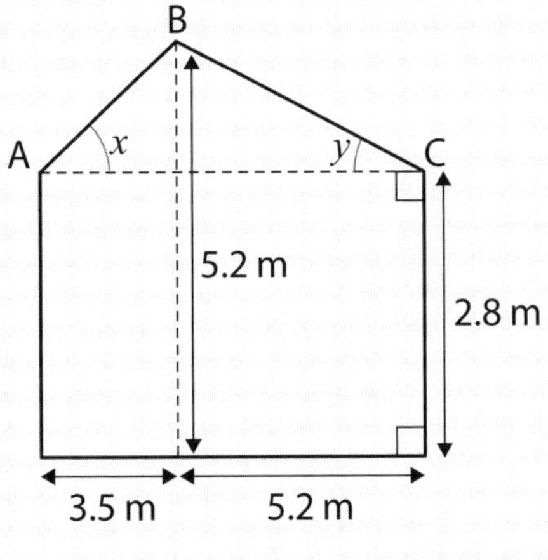

a What are the sizes of angles x and y?

x = ... y = ...

b What are the lengths of the roof at AB and BC?

AB = ... BC = ...

13 Graphs

13.1 Plotting coordinates

1 Find the mid point of the line segment between:

a (2, 8) and (8, 8) ....

b (−4, 5) and (−4, 1) ....

c (3, 2) and (3, −4) ....

d (−2, −5) and (−2, 3) ....

2 Find the mid point of the line segment between:

a (4, 0) and (0, 6) ....

b (−4, 0) and (0, 10) ....

c (5, 0) and (0, −4) ....

d (0, −5) and (−3, 0) ....

3 **a** Find the coordinates of the midpoint of AB.

....

b B is the midpoint of AD. Find the coordinates of D.

....

c C is the midpoint of AE. Find the coordinates of E.

....

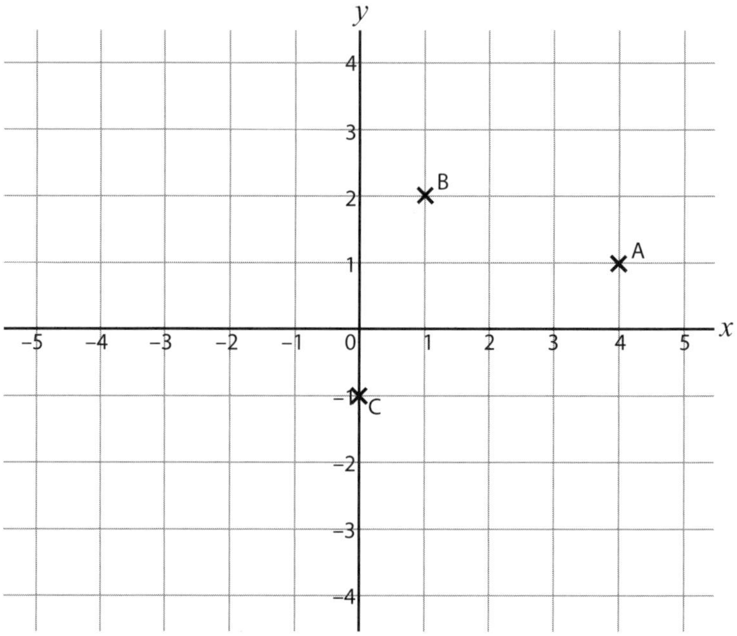

d A is the midpoint of BF. Find the coordinates of F. ....

4 The centre of a square is at (2, 1). One vertex is at (0, 4).

Draw the square on this coordinate grid.

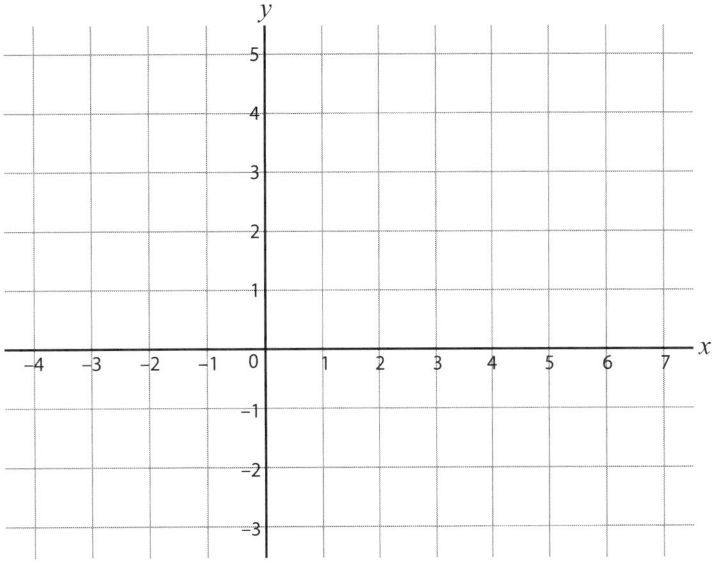

5 Two vertices of a square are (–2, 2) and (4, 2).

What are the coordinates of the other two vertices? Give all the possible answers.

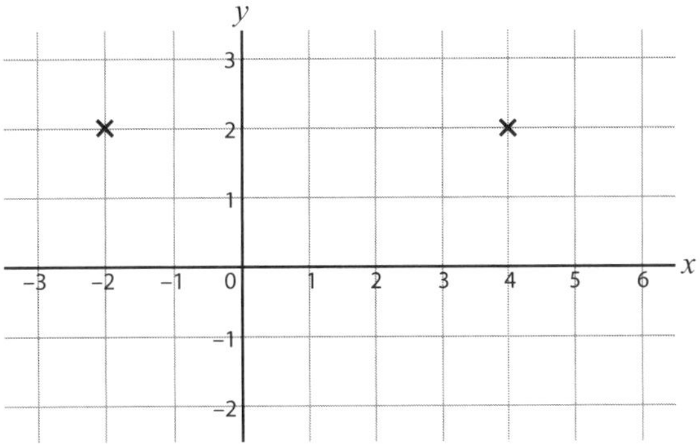

....

....

....

....

13.2 Other straight lines

1 These points are in a straight line. Write in the missing coordinates.

(5, 6) (–5, –4) (2, 3) (8, ...) (12, ...) (–3, ...) (–10, ...)

2 These points are in a straight line. Write in the missing coordinates.

(6, 0) (2, 4) (–1, 7) (0, ...) (5, ...) (–4, ...) (9, ...)

3 The equation of a line is $y = x + 4$.

State whether each of these points is on the line or not. Write YES or NO.

a (8, 12) .... **b** (−8, −12) ....

c (22, 18) .... **d** (−15, −11) ....

4 The equation of a line is $y = 3x - 5$.

State whether each of these points is on the line or not. Write YES or NO.

a (10, 5) .... **b** (7, 16) ....

c (−4, −7) .... **d** (−10, −35) ....

5 The equation of a line is $y = \frac{1}{4}x + 2$.

State whether each of these points is on the line or not. Write YES or NO.

a (12, 5) .... **b** (20, 7) ....

c (−8, 0) .... **d** $(-14, -1\frac{1}{2})$ ....

6 **a** Fill in this table of values.

x	4	2	0	−2	−4
$\frac{1}{4}x + 2$					

b Draw the line with the equation $y = \frac{1}{4}x + 2$ on this coordinate grid.

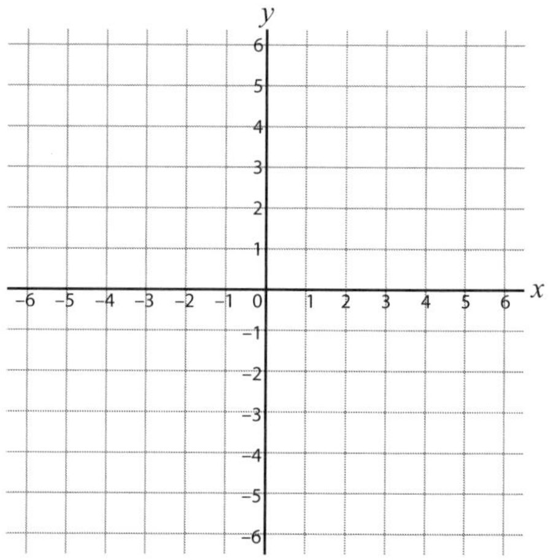

7 On the grid for Question 6, draw the line with the equation $y = \frac{1}{2}x - 2$.

8 Here are the equations of some lines.

For each one, find where it crosses the x-axis and the y-axis.

a $y = 2x - 6$ ....

b $y = 2x + 6$ ....

c $y = \frac{1}{2}x + 6$ ....

d $y = \frac{1}{2}x - 6$ ....

Mixed questions

1 Two opposite vertices of a square are (2, 4) and (–3, –1). They are at each end of a diagonal.

Write down the coordinates of the other two vertices.

.... and ....

2 One side of a rectangle goes from (7, 1) to (5, 5). The centre of the rectangle is at (2, 1).

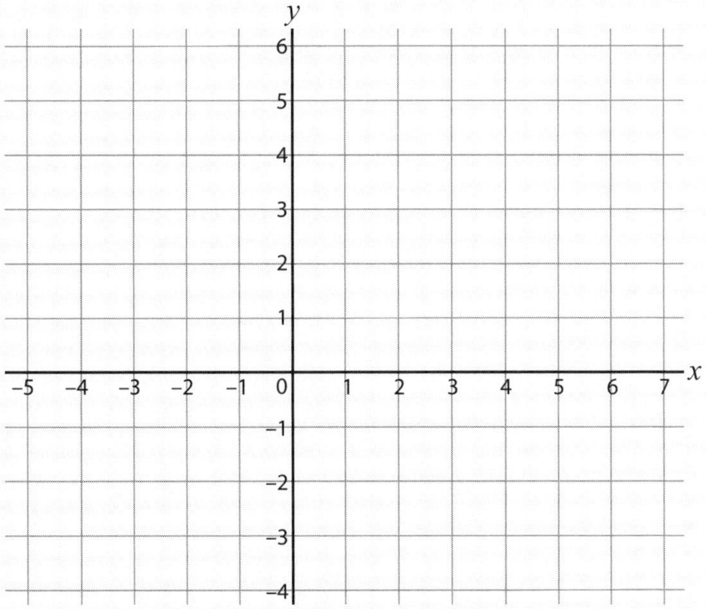

a Draw the rectangle on this coordinate grid.

b Write down the coordinates of the other two vertices.

....

and

....

3 Look at the four lines on the grid.

a Write the correct letter next to FOUR of these equations.

$y = x + 2$ ....

$y = x - 2$ ....

$y = 2x + 2$ ....

$y = \frac{1}{2}x + 2$ ....

$y = 2x - 2$ ....

$y = \frac{1}{2}x - 2$ ....

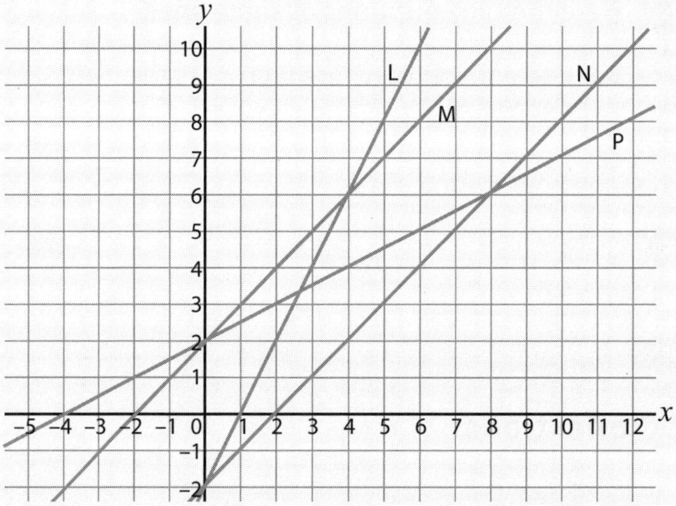

b Draw the two lines without a letter on the coordinate grid.

4 Work out the equations of these lines.

A ....

B ....

C ....

D ....

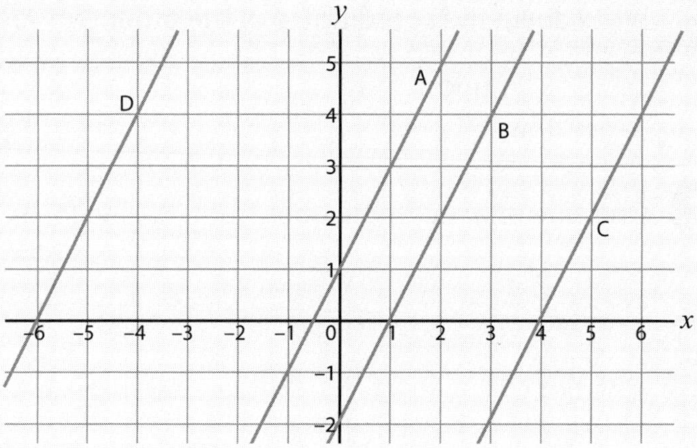

5 Work out the equations of these lines.

A ....

B ....

C ....

D ....

E ....

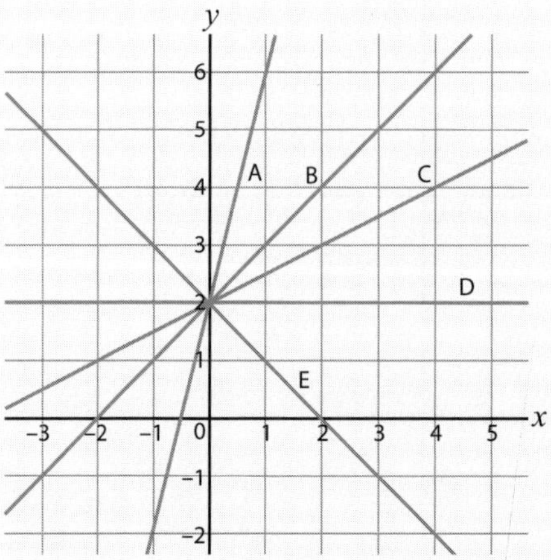

14 Ratio and proportion

14.1 Simplifying ratios

1 Write each ratio in its simplest form.

Make sure both quantities are in the same units before you simplify.

a 5 cm : 2 mm ....

b 2 kg : 250 g ....

c 1.2 l : 50 ml ....

d 2 days : 9 hours ....

2 Nia makes a fruit drink using 0.4 l of orange juice, 0.25 l of mango juice and 0.35 l of pineapple juice. Write the ratio of orange : mango : pineapple juice in its simplest form.

....

....

Change all quantities to ml before you simplify.

3 Rafina makes bread using $1\frac{1}{2}$ kg of flour. She uses 0.4 kg of rye flour and 250 g of buckwheat flour. The rest is white flour.

Write down the ratio of rye : buckwheat : white flour in its simplest form.

....

....

4 The bar chart shows the number of red, green and blue jumpers sold in a shop in one week. Write the ratio of red : green : blue jumpers sold in its simplest form.

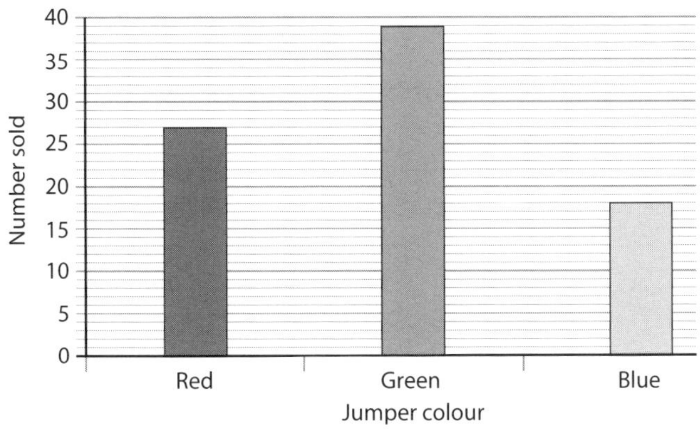

....

....

....

....

14.2 Sharing in a ratio

1 Brad has a jar containing 50 coins. He has 5-cent, 10-cent and 25-cent coins in the ratio 5 : 3 : 2.

a How many coins of each value does he have?

....

....

b How much money does he have in total?

....

2 Mia, Ewan and Dai raise a total of $432 for charity.

Mia raises twice as much as Ewan. Ewan raises five times as much as Dai.

How much do they each raise?

....

....

3 Ryan spends half of his pocket money on books and magazines in the ratio 4 : 1.

How much does he spend on books when he gets a total of $24 pocket money?

....

....

4 The graph shows the amount of yellow, blue and white paint in a 2-litre can of green paint.

How much blue paint is there in a 1.25-litre can of the same green paint?

....

....

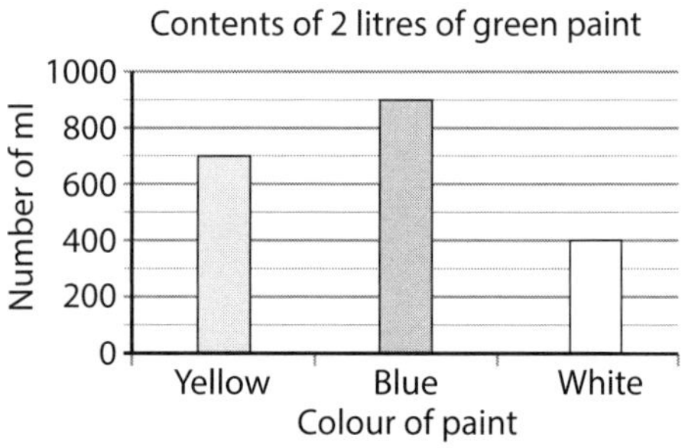

14.3 Using direct proportion

1 A shop has crisps on offer.

Offer 1	**Offer 2**	**Offer 3**
3 bags for 85 cents	7 bags for \$1.75	15 bags for \$3.99

Which offer is the best value for money? Explain your answer.

....

....

....

2 A businessman buys 30 t of rice for \$6300. He sells it for \$1.60 per kg.

How much profit does he make per kilogram?

....

....

Mixed questions

1 The mass of a curry is half beans, 35% lentils, $\frac{1}{10}$ fruit and the rest is sauce.

a Write down the ratio of beans : lentils : fruit : sauce in its simplest form.

....

....

b How many grams of lentils are in 800 g of curry?

....

....

2 You can estimate the height of a person if you know the distance around their head.

The ratio of distance around head : height is approximately 2 : 15.

a The distance around Taros' head is 18 cm. Approximately how tall is he?

....

....

b Hiri is 1.8 m tall. What is the approximate distance around her head?

....

....

c A burglar steals some jewellery from a house.
He accidently drops his hat during the burglary.

i What is the approximate height of the burglar?

....

....

ii Do you think it is a good idea for the police to be looking for a man who is the height you found in part i? Explain your answer.

....

....

....

15 Time

15.1 The 12-hour and 24-hour clock

1 How long is it from:

a 17:30 Saturday to 04:45 Sunday? ....

b 23:25 Monday to 10:10 Tuesday? ....

c 09:15 Tuesday to 12:50 Wednesday? ....

d 08:50 Friday to 19:30 Saturday? ....

2 Camilla travels to London. She leaves home at 09 50 and takes 4 hours 45 minutes to get there.

a What time does Camilla arrive? ....

Stanley also travels to London. His journey takes 2 hours 15 minutes. He arrives 25 minutes before Camilla.

b What time did Stanley leave home? ....

3 The clock below shows the times in different cities.

When it is 03:30 on Monday in Lagos, what day and time is it in:

a Beirut? ....

b Mumbai? ....

c New York? ....

Beirut	Hong Kong	Lagos	Mumbai	New York
14:50	19:50	12:50	17:20	07:50

4 When it is 09:25 in London, it is 16:25 in Shanghai.

A plane leaves London for Shanghai at 17:25 on Tuesday. The flight lasts 11 hours 10 minutes.

When does the plane arrive in Shanghai?

....

5 A plane leaves Amsterdam at 12:45 on Tuesday and arrives in Chicago at 14:15 the same day.

The plane leaves Chicago at 18:25 on Tuesday and arrives in Amsterdam at 09:55 on Wednesday.

The plane is in the air for the same length of time on each flight.

Work out the time difference between Amsterdam and Chicago.

....

15.2 Timetables

1 This timetable shows the departure times of three trains from Manchester.

Manchester	09:27	11:07	12:27
Birmingham	11:04	12:42	13:58
Bristol		13:05	
Reading	12:50		15:50
Bournemouth	14:11		17:11

How long is the journey from Manchester to:

a Bournemouth? ....

b Reading? ....

c Bristol? ....

2 This timetable shows times of flights from London to Doha on one day.

Depart London	Arrive Doha	Flight time
08:00	16:55	6 h 55 m
10:50	19:40	
15:05		6 h 50 m
16:00	00:45 + 1 day	
21:30		6 h 45 m
21:55		6 h 55 m

a Said misses the 15:05 from London. The next flight is full but there are seats on the flight after that. How long is it until the next available flight? ....

b Work out the time difference between London and Doha. ....

c Fill in the missing numbers in the table.

3 Gatwick and Stansted are two airports near London. This timetable shows the times of coaches from Gatwick to Stansted.

Gatwick depart	07:10	07:20	09:25	09:55
London coach station arrive		09:20		11:15
London coach station depart		10:10		11:45
Stansted arrive	10:25	11:50	12:25	13:15

a Work out the shortest journey time from Gatwick to Stansted. ....

b Work out the longest journey time from Gatwick to Stansted. ....

c On two of the journeys you have to change coaches. How long is the shortest wait between coaches? ....

d Ayesha is travelling from Gatwick to Stansted. Her plane leaves Stansted at 14:05. She wants to arrive at least two hours before her plane leaves. What is the latest time she can leave Gatwick by coach? ....

15.3 Real-life graphs

1 This graph shows a car journey.

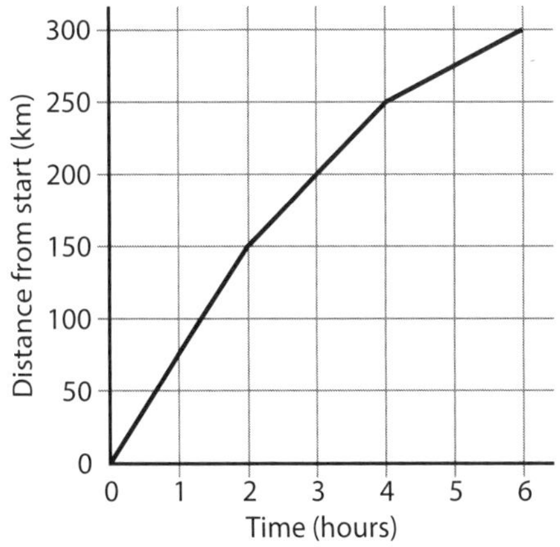

a Show that the average speed for the first two hours is 75 km/h.

....

....

The average speed for a journey is the total distance divided by the total time. If the distance is in kilometres and the time is in hours, then the speed is in kilometres per hour (km/h).

b Show that the average speed for the second two hours is 50 km/h.

....

c Find the average speed for the final two hours.

....

d How many hours does the whole journey take? ......

e Work out the average speed for the whole journey. ...... km/h

2 This graph shows the journey of a cyclist.

The journey is in two parts, with a rest in the middle.

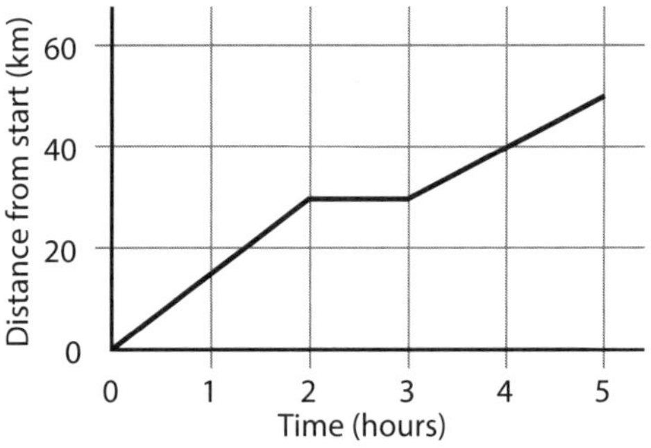

a Find the average speed for the first two hours. ....

b Find the average speed for the final two hours. ....

c Find the average speed for the whole journey. ....

3 This is the graph of a journey.

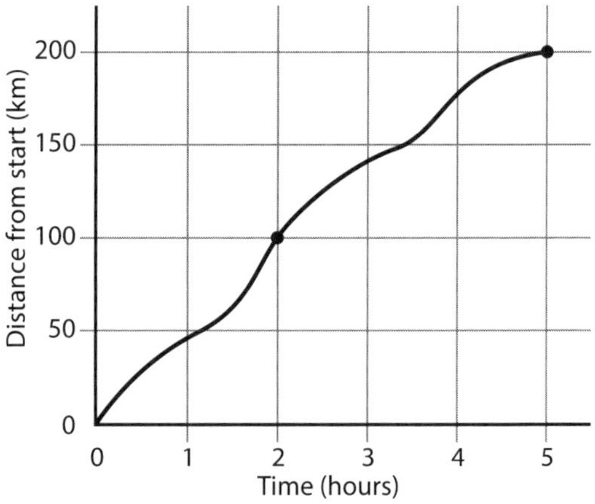

a Find the average speed for the first two hours. ...... km/h

b Find the average speed for the last three hours. ...... km/h

c Find the average speed for the whole journey. ...... km/h

Mixed questions

1 Moscow is 2 hours ahead of London and 4 hours behind Jakarta.

Mexico City is 6 hours behind London and 10 hours behind Karachi.

Complete this table of equivalent times.

Jakarta	Karachi	London	Mexico City	Moscow
	20:22			

2 A flight from London to Auckland takes 27 hours 30 minutes.

London is 11 hours behind Auckland.

A plane leaves London for Auckland at 18:20 on Sunday 3 March.

Work out when it arrives in Auckland.

....

3 A walk starts at 09:30 and finishes at 14:30. The length of the walk is 30 km.

Work out the average speed. ...... km/h

4 Here is a train timetable.

Ashton	09:30	11:50	13:15
Beesley	10:25	12:55	
Carton	11: 42	03:02	
Deptford	13:05	15:25	
Easton	16:21	18:41	

a How long is the journey from Ashton to Easton? ....

b How long is the journey from Beesley to Deptford? ....

c A train leaves Ashton at 13:15. Assuming that the journey times are the same, fill in the missing times in the timetable.

16 Probability

16.1 Equally likely outcomes

1 A computer randomly generates a single digit in the range 0 to 9.

Work out the probability that the digit is:

a odd .... **b** 9 .... **c** not 9 ....

2 A computer randomly generates two digits to produce a number in the range 00 to 99.

Work out the probability that:

a both the digits are 9 ....

b neither of the digits is 9 ....

c exactly one of the digits is 9 ....

3 A computer randomly generates three digits to produce a number in the range 000 to 999.

Work out the probability that:

a all three digits are 9 ....

b exactly two of the digits are 9 ....

c none of the digits is 9 ....

d exactly one of the digits is 9 ....

4 A fair dice has 12 faces. There is a number on each face.

When the dice is thrown, the probability of scoring 2 is $\frac{1}{2}$, the probability of scoring 4 is $\frac{1}{4}$ and the probability of scoring 6 is $\frac{1}{6}$.

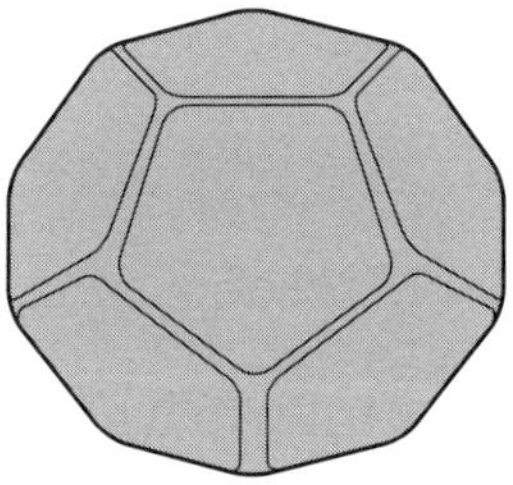

What can you say about the numbers on the dice?

....

....

16.2 Estimating probabilities

1 Tomas catches a bus to work each morning.

He keeps a record for 30 days and finds that the bus is late on 9 days.

a Find the experimental probability that the bus is:

i late .... **ii** on time ....

In the next 20 days the bus is late 4 times.

b Use the results for all 50 days to find the experimental probability that the bus is:
i late .... **ii** on time ....

c Tomas catches the bus 186 times in a year.

Estimate how many days the bus will be late. Explain how you get your answer.

....

....

....

2 Karim uses a spreadsheet to model the throws of a dice.

He records the total number of 6s after each 10 throws.

This table show his results.

Total throws	10	20	30	40	50	60	70	80	90	100
Number of 6s	2	2	3	3	4	6	9	12	14	16

a Complete this table to show the experimental probability of a 6 after 10, 20, 30, etc. throws.

Total throws	10	20	30	40	50	60	70	80	90	100
Probability	0.2	0.1			0.08					

b Plot the experimental probabilities on this graph.

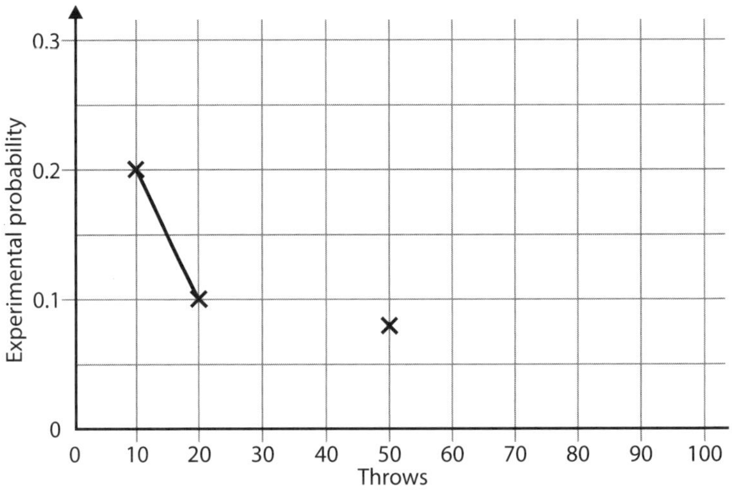

c What do you think the graph will look like if Karim models more throws on the computer?

....

....

....

....

....

3 Some students are asked if they want to be engineers, lawyers or accountants.

The results are shown in this table.

	Number in survey	Want to be		
		Engineer	Lawyer	Accountant
Girls	80	12	20	16
Boys	120	48	18	20

a What is the probability that a girl wants to be:

i an engineer? .... **ii** a lawyer? .... **iii** an accountant? ....

b What is the probability that a boy wants to be:

i an engineer? .... **ii** a lawyer? .... **iii** an accountant? ....

c Taking all the students together, what is the probability that a student wants to be:

i an engineer? .... **ii** a lawyer?............ **iii** an accountant?............

Mixed questions

1 A bag contains a number of coloured balls. One ball is taken out at random.

The probability that the ball is red is $\frac{1}{3}$.

The probability that the ball is blue is $\frac{2}{5}$.

a Work out the smallest possible number of balls in the bag. ....

The probability that the ball is yellow is $\frac{1}{6}$.

b What is now the smallest possible number of balls in the bag? ....

The rest of the balls are green.

c Work out the probability of taking out a green ball. ....

2 The probability that Ahmed gets up late is 0.2.

The probability that Beth gets up late is 0.35.

a Are these events mutually exclusive? ....

b Work out the probability that Ahmed does not get up late. ....

These probabilities are based on recording whether or not they were late getting up for a period of 40 days.

c Work out how many days Ahmed and Beth got up late in those 40 days.

Ahmed: ...... days

Beth: ...... days

3 United are a football team.

The probability that United will win their next match is 0.55.

The probability that United will win or draw their next match is 0.85.

Work out the probability that in the next match United will:

a lose .... **b** draw ....

4 Here are ten cards. Each card has a letter and a number.

X1	Y2	X3	X1	Y1
X3	Y2	X1	Y2	X1

Dita takes a card at random.

a Work out the probability that it has on it:

i 1 .... **ii** Y and 2 ....

iii X .... **iv** 1 or 3 ....

b Say whether these pairs of events are mutually independent. Circle YES or NO.

i	Dita's card has an X	Dita's card has a Y	YES	NO
ii	Dita's card has an X	Dita's card has a 3	YES	NO
iii	Dita's card has an Y	Dita's card has a 3	YES	NO
iv	Dita's card has an X	Dita's card has a 2	YES	NO

17.1 Reflecting shapes

1 On the grid:

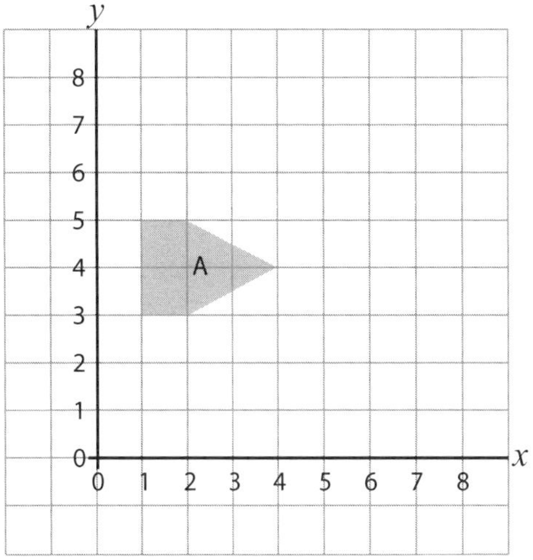

a Reflect shape A in the line $y = x$. Label the new shape B.

> The line $y = x$ is the diagonal line that goes through the points (0, 0) and (8, 8).

b Reflect shape B in the line $y = 4$. Label the new shape C.

c Reflect shape C in the line $y = x$. Label the new shape D.

d What is the order of rotation of the complete shape? ....

e How many lines of symmetry does the complete shape have? ....

2 The diagram shows triangle $A_1 B_1 C_1$.

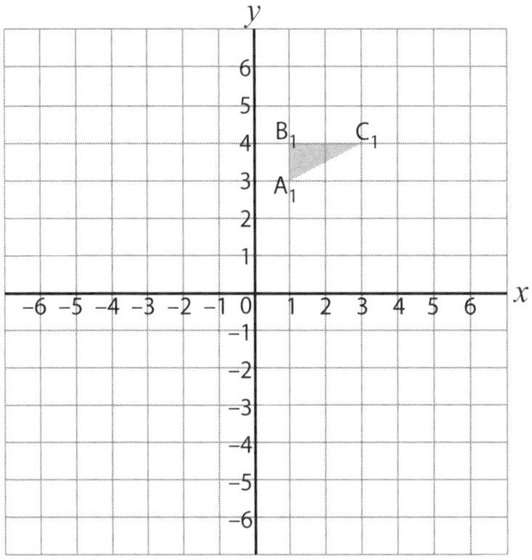

a **i** Reflect triangle $A_1 B_1 C_1$ in the line $y = x$. Label the new triangle $A_2 B_2 C_2$.

ii Complete the table showing the coordinates of the vertices of the two triangles.

Object $A_1 B_1 C_1$	A_1	(1, 3)	B_1		C_1	
Image $A_2 B_2 C_2$	A_2		B_2		C_2	

What do you notice about the coordinates of the object and its image?

....

....

b i Draw another shape on to the grid.

ii Make a table, like the one in part a), and predict the coordinates of the vertices of the image of your shape after a reflection in the line $y = x$.

iii Now draw the reflection of your shape in the line $y = x$ and check that your predicted coordinates are correct.

c i On the grid opposite, draw a reflection of $A_1 B_1 C_1$ in the line $y = -x$.

Label the new triangle $A_3 B_3 C_3$.

ii Complete the table showing the coordinates of the vertices of the two triangles.

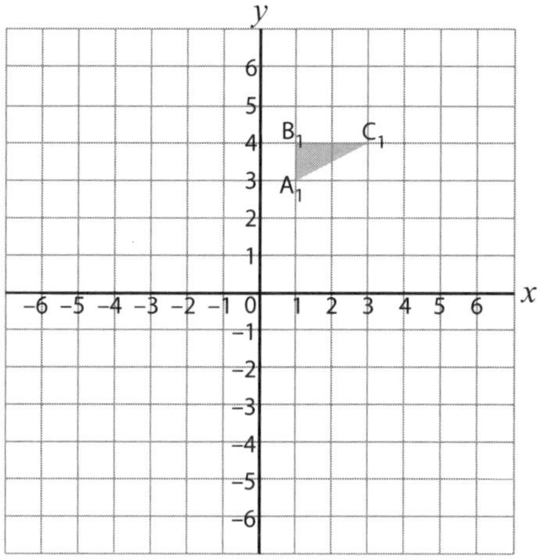

Object $A_1 B_1 C_1$	A_1		B_1		C_1	
Image $A_3 B_3 C_3$	A_3		B_3		C_3	

iii What do you notice about the coordinates of the object and its image?

....

....

d i Draw another shape on the grid.

ii Make a table, like the one in part c), and predict the coordinates of the vertices of the image of your shape after a reflection in the line $y = -x$.

iii Now draw the reflection of your shape in the line $y = -x$ and check that your predicted coordinates are correct.

17.2 Rotating shapes

1 **a** On the grid, draw a rotation of shape A, 90° clockwise about centre (3, 3). Label the image B.

b On the grid, draw a rotation of shape B, 180° about centre (3, 4). Label the image C.

c On the grid, draw a rotation of shape C, 90° anticlockwise about centre (6, 4). Label the image D.

d Describe the ROTATION that takes shape A directly to shape D.

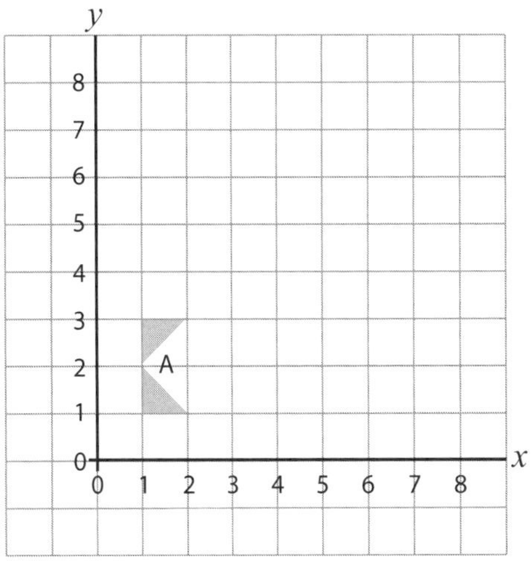

....

....

e Describe the REFLECTION that takes shape A directly to shape D.

....

....

2 On each of these diagrams:

i Mark with a dot the centre of rotation.

ii Describe the rotation that takes shape A to shape B.

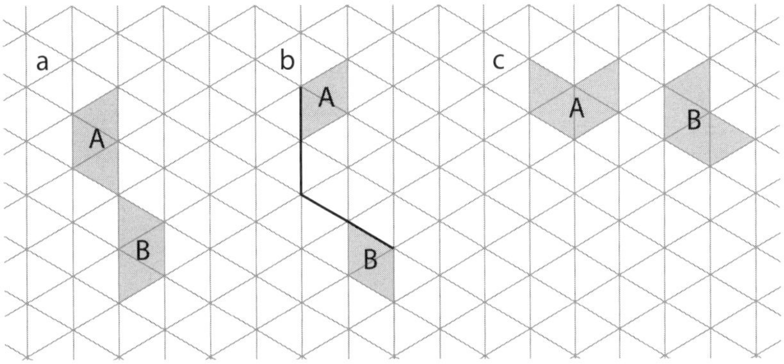

....

....

....

17.3 Translating shapes

1 **a** Patsun translates a shape 2 squares left and 4 squares up. He then translates the image 7 squares right and 3 squares down.

What single translation has the same effect as these two translations combined?

b Junior translates a shape 5 squares left and 2 squares down.

What translation must she now do on the image so that the combined effect of both translations is a single transformation of 3 squares right and 1 square up?

2 In a game of chess, in one turn, a knight can move either 1 square left or right followed by 2 squares up or down OR 2 squares left or right followed by 1 square up or down. On the chess board opposite, the K shows the position of the knight.

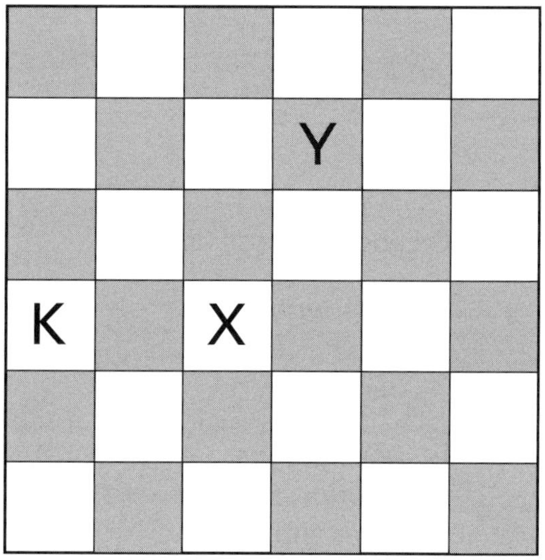

a **i** Describe the translations that the knight has to make to end up on the square marked X.

ii What is the least number of moves that the knight can make to get from K to X?

b **i** Describe the translations that the knight has to make to end up on the square marked Y.

....

....

....

ii What is the least number of moves that the knight can make to get from K to Y?

....

....

Mixed questions

1 **a** On the grid, draw the image of triangle A after a rotation of 180^0 about centre (3, 3). Label the image B.

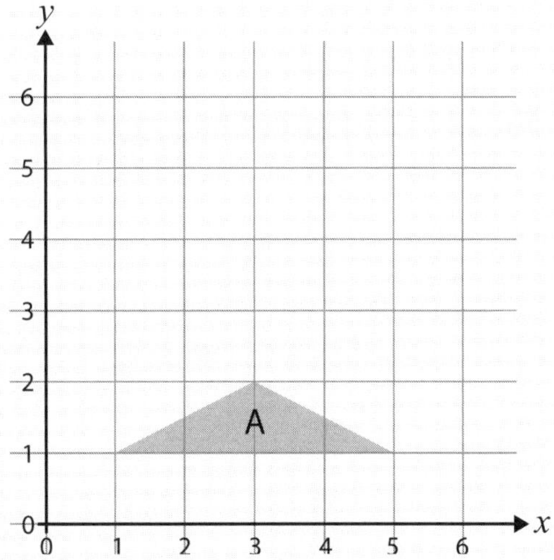

b Describe two different transformations that would take triangle B to triangle A.

Transformation 1: ....

....

Transformation 2: ....

....

2 The diagram shows shape C.

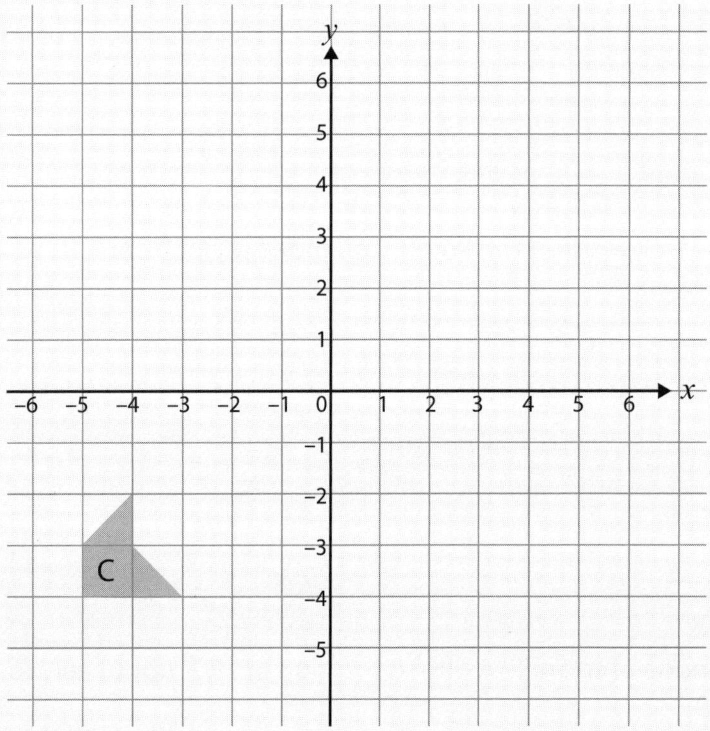

a Draw the image of shape C after a reflection in the line $x = -1$. Label the image D.

b Draw the image of shape D after a translation of 2 squares right and 1 square up. Label the image E.

c Draw the image of shape E after a rotation of 180^0 about centre (0, 1). Label the image F.

d Describe the single transformation that will take shape F to shape C.

....

....

e Describe the single transformation that will take shape D to shape F.

....

....

18 Area, perimeter and volume

18.1 Converting between units for area

1 Adam says that $8\ cm^2$ is the same as $80\ mm^2$ because there are 10 mm in 1 cm.

Explain why he is wrong.

....

....

2 Work out the answers to the following. Give each answer in:

i mm^2 **ii** cm^2

a $8\ cm^2 + 150\ mm^2$

....

....

b $12.25\ cm^2 - 950\ mm^2$

....

....

3 Work out the answers to the following. Give each answer in:

i cm^2 **ii** m^2

a $0.25\ m^2 + 12\,000\ cm^2$

....

....

b $595\,000\ cm^2 - 12.3\ m^2$

....

....

4 Dinesh has a piece of wood with an area of $1.6\,m^2$. He cuts it into five pieces of equal area.

What is the area of each piece in:

a m^2 **b** cm^2

....

....

....

18.2 Calculating the area and perimeter of rectangles

1 A beach volleyball court has a length of 16 m. The area of the court is $128\,m^2$.

What is the perimeter of the court?

....

....

....

2 The Willis Tower in Chicago has a square base. The perimeter of the base is 274.4 m.

What is the area of the base?

....

....

....

3 Work out the area of these rectangles.

Remember to give the units with your answers.

a

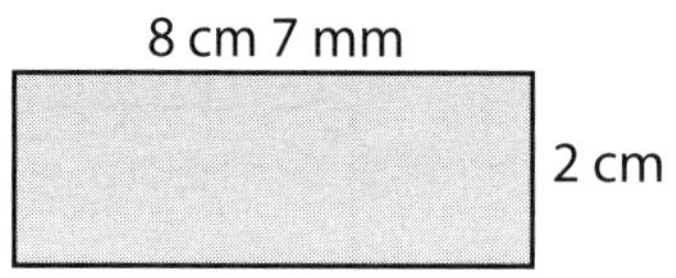

....

....

b

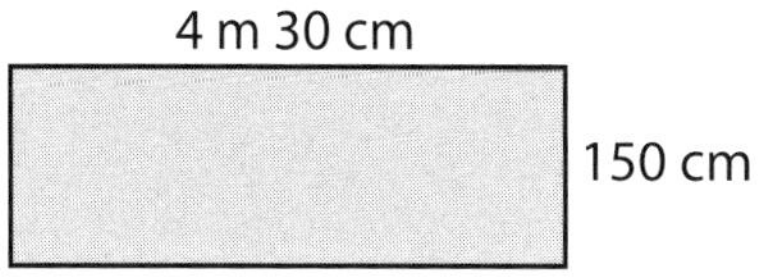

....

....

....

18.3 Calculating the area and perimeter of compound shapes

1 Work out the area of these compound shapes.

a

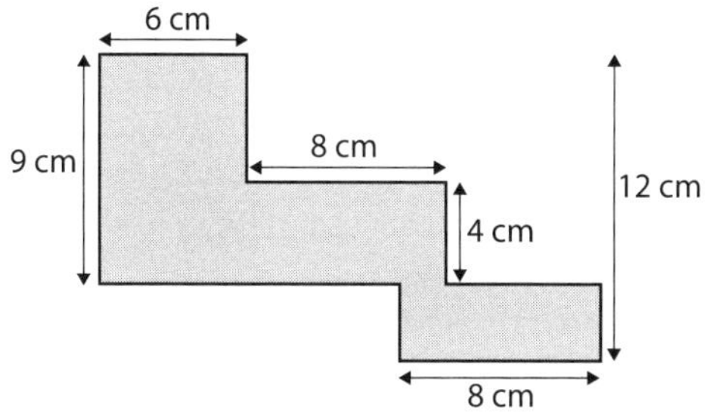

....

....

....

....

b

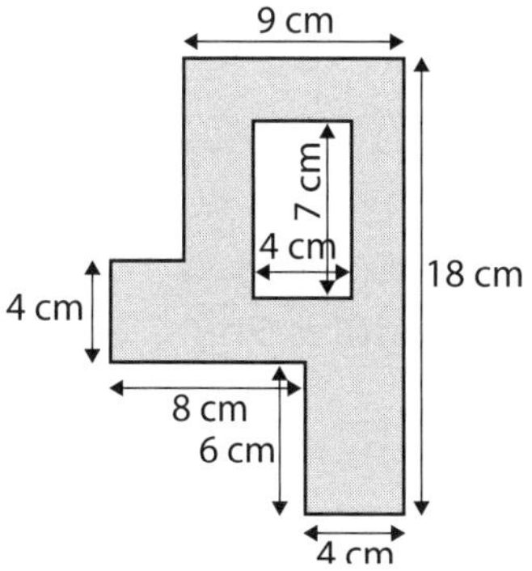

....

....

....

....

2 This shape has an area of $216\,cm^2$.

Work out the missing length.

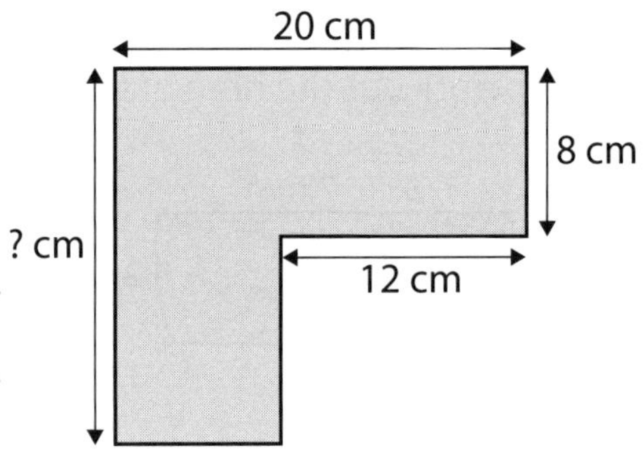

....

....

....

....

18.4 Calculating the volume of cuboids

1 A cube has a volume of $216\,cm^3$.

What is the side length of the cube?

....

....

2 **a** What is the volume of this cuboid?

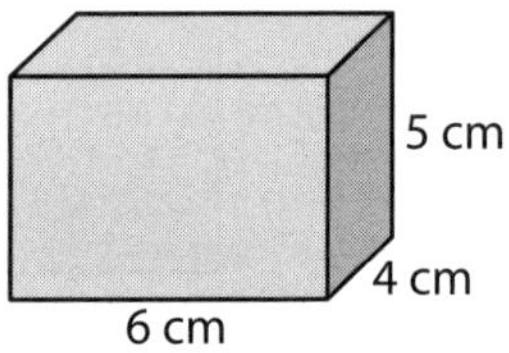

....

....

b Write down the dimensions of four other cuboids that have the same volume.

....

....

3 A cuboid has a volume of $420\,mm^3$. The length is 12 mm, the width is 5 mm.

What is the height of the cuboid?

....

....

18.5 Calculating the surface area of cubes and cuboids

1 Work out the surface area of a cube with side length 0.08 m.

Give your answer in cm^2.

....

....

....

....

2 A cuboid has a length of 15 cm, a width of 0.2 m and a height of 12 mm.

Work out the surface area of the cuboid in cm^2.

....

....

....

....

3 Raul wants to paint the inside and outside of this open box.

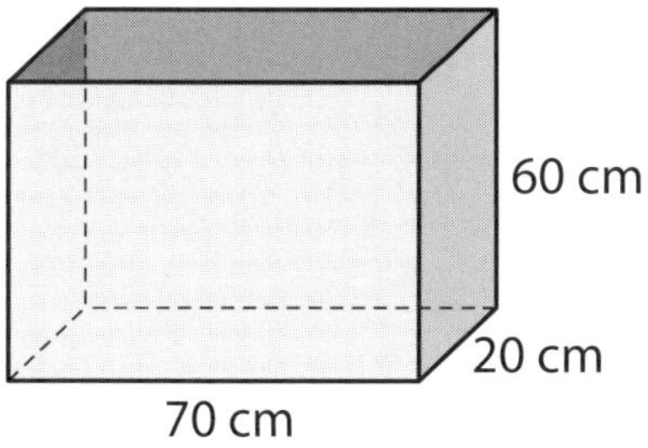

An open box is a box with no lid.

He has enough paint to cover 30 000 cm^2.
Does he have enough paint to paint the box?

Show all your working.

....

....

....

....

Mixed questions

1 A rectangle has a perimeter of 40 cm and an area of 51 cm^2.

What are the length and width of the rectangle?

....

....

....

....

2 These solid shapes are made from cuboids. Calculate the volume of each solid shape.

a

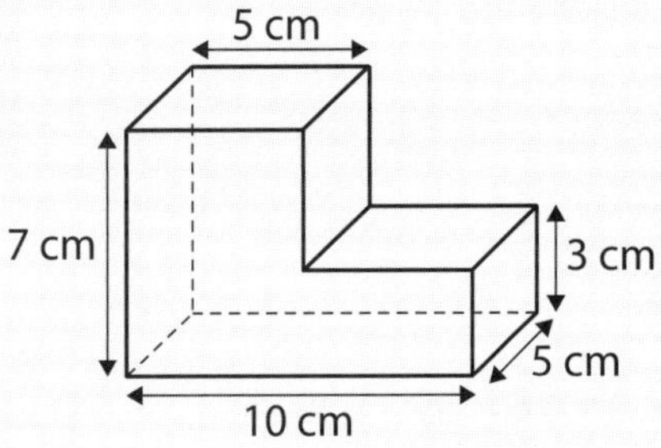

....

....

....

....

b

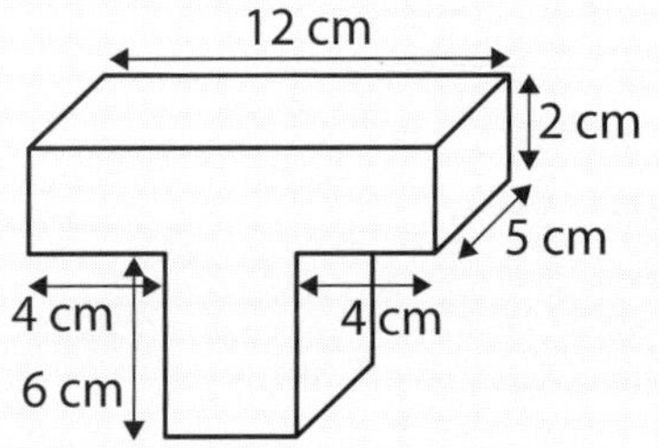

....

....

....

....

3 These three boxes have the same volume.

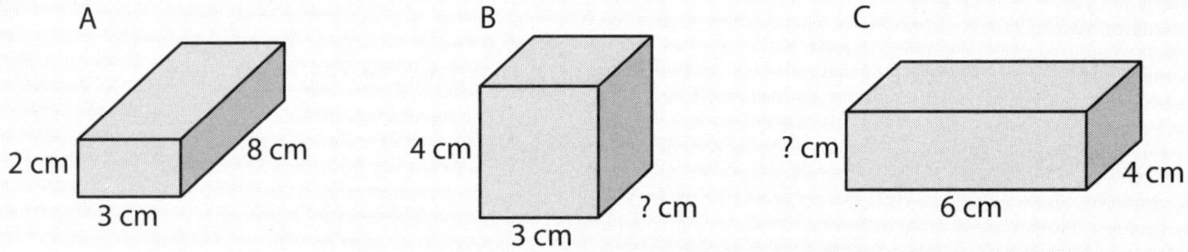

a Work out the missing lengths.

....

....

b Work out the surface area of each cuboid.

....

....

....

....

c If you ran a business that needed to make a box with this volume, would you rather buy box A, B or C? Explain your answer.

....

....

d These are the dimensions of three boxes that have a volume of $64\,cm^3$.

D 4 cm by 4 cm by 4 cm **E** 2 cm by 8 cm by 4 cm **F** 1 cm by 4 cm by 16 cm

Which box do you think will have the:

i largest surface area? **ii** smallest surface area?

Explain your answers. Work out the surface area of each cuboid, then check to see if your answers to i) and ii) were correct.

....

....

....

....

....

....

....

....

....

....

....

....

19 Interpreting and discussing results

19.1 Interpreting and drawing pictograms, bar charts, bar-line graphs and frequency diagrams

1 Yolo asked 30 people their favourite flavour of milkshake out of vanilla (V), strawberry (S) and chocolate (C). Her results are shown below.

V	S	S	V	C	S	C	V	S	S
S	C	V	C	S	S	V	S	C	C
S	S	S	V	V	S	S	S	V	S

a Complete the tally chart.

Flavour	Tally	Frequency
Vanilla		
Strawberry		
Chocolate		
	Total	

b Draw a pictogram to show Yolo's results. Remember to include a key.

2 Shen timed how long it took some students to solve a puzzle. The times, in seconds, are shown below.

20	43	32	34	12	30	22	33	36	42	40	24
40	35	45	42	31	30	39	41	29	37	38	31
33	14	33	28	41	39	14	36	37	46	45	25
21	35	43	34	31	15	39	45	38	18	22	19
41	26	32	13	46	29	43	23	27	40	43	30

a How many students were timed?

....

b Complete the grouped tally chart.

Time (seconds)	Tally	Frequency
10–19		
20–29		
30–39		
40–49		
	Total	

c Draw a frequency diagram to show the information.

19.2 Interpreting and drawing pie charts

1 The table shows the percentage sales of different coloured T-shirts in a shop in one month.

Colour	Red	Blue	Yellow	Green
Percentage	35%	40%	10%	15%

Draw a pie chart to show this information.

19.3 Drawing conclusions

1 The frequency diagrams show the number of brothers of the students in classes 7T and 7P.

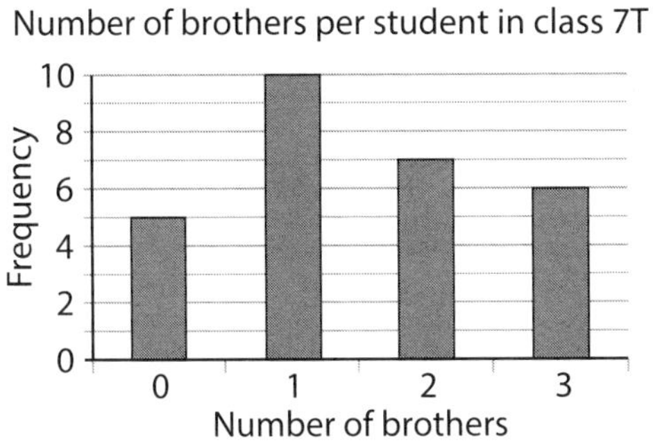

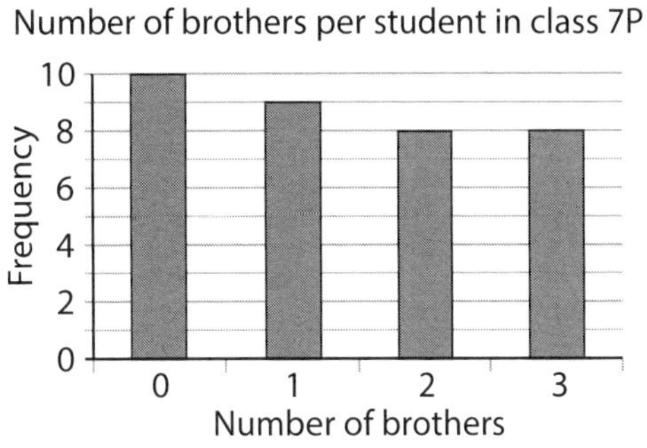

a Compare the frequency diagrams and make two comments.

....

....

b Work out how many students there are in:

i Class 7T ....

ii Class 7P ....

c Work out the total number of brothers in:

i Class 7T ....

ii Class 7P ....

d Work out the mean number of brothers per student in:

i Class 7T ....

ii Class 7P ....

e Compare and comment on the mean number of brothers per student in classes 7T and 7P.

....

....

Mixed questions

1 The pictogram shows the amount of money John raised for a charity.

The bar graph shows how much money Raul raised for the same charity.

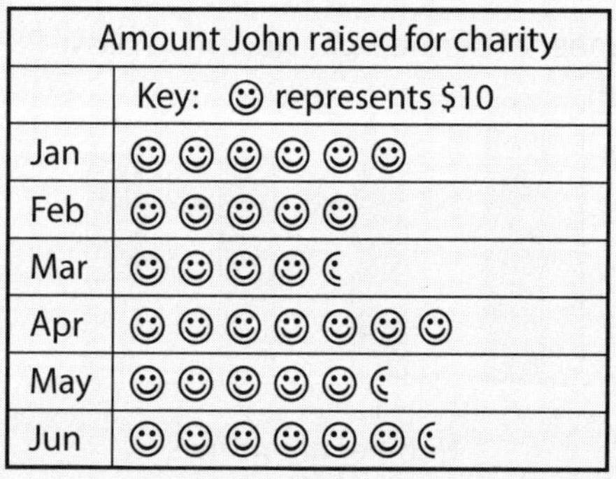

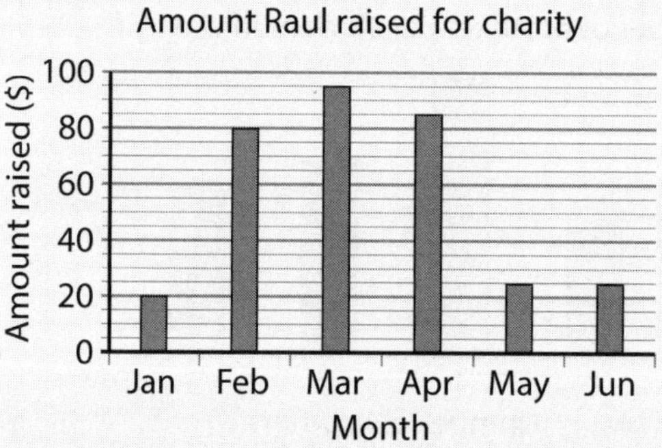

a Work out the mean amount raised per month by:

i John ....

....

ii Raul ....

....

b Work out the range in the amount raised each month by:

i John ....

ii Raul ....

c Write a short paragraph comparing the two charts. Include your answers to a) and b).

....

....

....

....

....

....

....

....

Notes

Notes

Notes

Notes